SISTER SIREN

SISTER SIREN

A NON FICTION ABOUT ADDICTION

MICHAELA K. CANTERBURY

A Field Guide On How To Love An Addict

KELLEYBURY PRESS

Published by Kelleybury Press

For more information or to contact the author, go to: MKCanterbury.com/

ISBN (paperback): 979-8-9867237-0-9
ISBN (ebook): 979-8-9867237-1-6

Cover art: ronniechua, https://ronniechua.myportfolio.com
Edited by Valerie Costa, Costa Creative Services
Cover and interior design by Christy Day, www.constellationbookservices.com

Printed in the United States of America

To Aunties

DISCLAIMER

This publication contains the opinions, ideas, and stories of its author. It is intended to provide helpful and informative materials on the subjects addressed in the publication. It is sold with the understanding that the author is not rendering medical or legal services or advice in this book. The reader should consult his or her own medical or legal professionals before adopting anything from this book or drawing inferences from it. This book is not intended to serve as a basis for any medical or legal advice, recommendation or decision of a specific protocol or strategy. The author specifically disclaims all responsibility for any liability, loss or risk personal or otherwise which is incurred as a consequence directly or indirectly of the use and application of any contents of this book.

Contents

About the Title

IN MYTHOLOGY, SIRENS ARE HALF BIRD, HALF WOMAN creatures that lure people to their deaths with seductive songs. Human demise occurs when the Sirens refrain penetrates the mortal's capacity to process the Sirens fatal melodic composition. Modern day Sirens have evolved, and continue to express what is difficult for the human spirit to process and endure.

Tales of Sirens include male warriors Odysseus and Orpheus. Odysseus overcame the Sirens' songs with a directive to his mates to tie him to the ships mast; with an order not to release him and instruction that his comrades plug their ears with wax to safely sail by the island where Sirens resided. Orpheaus was a musician, singer, and poet that sang louder than the Sirens to escape demise.

Muses are creatures that have the ability to overcome the Sirens' penetrating song with their own reprise. Muses and Sirens are two sides of the same coin; they are related and sing the same songs differently. The Muses' ballads are blessed with grace-filled gifts of exhortation that nourish, empower and energize. The Muses' melody diffuses a Sirens' penetratingly keen trill with high frequency faith that vibrates hope and encouragement to melancholy mortals that show up and witness the dark and scary places of the material world.

This book calls to those modern-day warriors summoned to underlie the lives of those they love unconditionally and suffer in an age of opiate and drug dependence that has become an epidemic and existential crisis. Contemporary combatants of this war on drugs must possess heart, strength, faith, and powerful unconditional love to overcome the painful songs sung by today's Sirens on the earthly and spiritual journeys the devil of addiction takes them on. It is my hope that the accounts in this book shine light on the dark, misunderstood and misguided areas of addiction and recovery, conjures courage and instills strength for those called to step into the world of substance use and abuse disorders with compassion, unyielding, everlasting, and eternal love.

Prologue
By Kaylen Kelley

I WAS ASLEEP, DOPE SICK, AND HAD A GNARLY INFECTION that was spreading through my body due to a huge abscess that had been festering on the back of my leg right at the knee pit. (Yes, it was the worst place ever for a giant, hot, festering infection. So gross.) I also had many other abscesses that freckled my body in varying states of infection. So I wasn't in great shape, to say the least, and my attitude and mood reflected the miserable experience that I was having.

I heard my name being called in my tortured, restless waking sleep that I had been in and out of for hours, waiting for the plug to come through. I had been lost in sleep purgatory for hours, not asleep but not fully awake, having the same disorienting, confusing and fragmented dreams on repeat. It was as if I had been planted in some delusional, drug-fueled writer's incomplete novel where none of the chapters have been finished and every one hundred words a sentence has been removed, so you have a vague idea of what's going on but can't be totally sure and you have to fill it in yourself. This anxiety-fueled half sleep fever dream is one of the cursed experiences that junkies become accustomed to while on their opiate addiction roller coaster, and it becomes a motivator that causes constant anxiety because the hell of withdrawals is always just in the background of the mind.

I heard my name and didn't immediately react; I was just glad that something new was finally happening in my anxiety dream. Then I heard my name again, followed by more indistinct yelling and some-thing hitting my window. I sat up and tried to orient myself while leaning over to open my window, which was really hard because I felt impossibly weak. I got it open just in time to hear "Your sister is coming in the house!" Those words computed just as I saw the top of my big sissy's head bob into sight from where I was sitting on my cot.

I knew right away it was too late. She was going to see it all; she was going to see so much. I know that I must have looked like hell, not like the little sister she had known for 36 years. The person she had cared for, guided, loved, encouraged, and watched grow up over the years. I knew she had seen me looking rough, especially over the previous three years. Even though I tried to cover up and pull myself together when I knew I would be seeing my family, I knew that over the years my sister had seen the abscesses, the bruises, the pock marks all over my body, along with my dull skin and hair, because it's impossible to hide it all. An addict that has really let go, given up and sank into the lifestyle has a look to them, and it really has little to do with all of the obvious and tangible things. You can see that their light has gone out; they are dulled, flat and are missing that intangible spark that living humans have. Drug addiction is the real zombie apocalypse and the human race is losing the battle right now.

My sister was at the top of the stairs and I moved faster than I had in a long while, knowing that I needed to do damage control by keeping her out of the bedrooms and getting her out of the house as fast as possible. At first I tried to play it off, even though I was wearing shorts and looked like the junkie version of that old comic strip character Cathy, with the same frenetic anxious energy. My sister was looking around gathering information and I wasn't sure if she was looking for hope or looking for confirmation of her fears. I already knew there wasn't much hope in this (trap) house.

Playing it off didn't last long and things started to spiral. I could hardly stand, I was limping around and wouldn't turn my back to her and I was grimacing in pain constantly. My sister saw it all. She asked me if I was okay and if she could help, did I need her to take me to the hospital, what was wrong, what was going on, was I okay? I was feeling overwhelmed and just needed to get her out of the house so she wasn't exposed to this disgusting, terrifying, hopeless, worthless rock bottom. She was so out of place, and that was too painful for me to handle. I was angry, yelling, screaming, telling her to leave, telling her she had to get out and just leave me alone. She was crying and pleading with me to just go with her. She said I needed help, I was in pain, I had an infection and was obviously sick. I spit venom and anger, but even in that moment I knew that I wasn't mad at her. I just didn't want her to see me like that, to see that place, but really I didn't want her to be exposed to it. I didn't want her to see things that she would never be able to unsee or forget. I can't remember how we left things. I sank down onto my broken cot for a moment and then started to dig around in my things for a fix, and just like some sort of dark magic . . . I found a stash. I made a shot and let it all go.

That is one of my most painful, shame filled, heavy memories and it was certainly my rock bottom moment for our relationship. Why am I sharing this? Why in the prologue of my sister's book, where she shares her experiences and personal journey of moving through addiction and eventually into recovery? The most powerful way to spread hope is through the real stories that life can get better. At that moment I didn't think I could get better, I didn't believe our relationship could come back from that place, and I couldn't even think about it. I felt so hopeless, so lost, so ashamed of myself, so lonely, and I didn't know who I was anymore.

Sometimes our most painful experiences become the catalyst for the change we need in our lives. It can be a slow process, like the pain planted the seed and then in the darkness a sprout grows. It takes time, patience and hope; all of which are hard to come by when you are in the eye of the storm of addiction. And other times, the painful experience is so intense and the feelings, realizations, loss and guilt act as the defibrillator that brings you back to life and gets you into action.

This experience planted such a seed, and I couldn't get it out of my head no matter how much I used, no matter who I was with, no matter what I did. The experience would replay in my head and the feelings I had were the water for that seed. It created a slight openness to change and awareness that I was getting closer to being ready. This thinking wasn't overt most of the time, but it was happening. So when I was assaulted by my landlord, I was already ready to get out of the drug lifestyle and change my life.

And that's just what I did. I called two people after I was assaulted and needed help, and of course my sister was one of those people. And just as she always had been, she was there for me when I needed her and she supported me when I needed it most. She was there for me as I navigated getting clean . . . again. She showed up guarded with boundaries but supportive, and that's what I needed. As I really showed up for myself and my recovery, her guard lowered, trust was slowly rebuilt and the boundaries shifted. I grew and healed and our relationship also grew and healed.

So here we are three years, two months, and a few days clean, and my sister has asked me to write the prologue to her book. A book she has put so much time, effort, energy, soul and heart into. This book that is so much more than simply a book, but a journey of healing, forgiveness, transformation, and, of course, hope. I'll be honest, when she first asked me if she could write this book I felt sick; like I was going to barf. Then I felt undeserving, unworthy, and just not good enough. I started to free fall into the shame spiral and went through all the reasons I couldn't do it, shouldn't do it, and why I was just a terrible, awful, shitty, broken, defective person that has caused too much pain and damage to be honored or included in such an awesome experience.

Why should I take up air time and space in her book where she is sharing her experiences of being hurt, manipulated, abused, disrupted, and repeatedly trampled on by an addict?

This addict.

I felt that this kind of honor should go to someone who didn't wreak such pain, havoc and chaos on our family.

I felt that there had to be someone more well-equipped and more deserving of such a special and important task.

Then I took a moment of pause.

I took a conscious and intentional breath.

I centered myself and I realigned myself to see this through the eyes of someone in recovery, as opposed to seeing it through the eyes of an addict.

Those two perspectives are significantly different.

When I look at this opportunity, this gift, through the eyes of a woman in long term recovery, I own that I am worthy.

I see that I am deserving.

And I recognize that I do have a lot to offer.

I own and know that I am the best person to write the prologue for the story of my sister's account of what it was like for her as she was loving, supporting, being hurt by, and living with this addict.

Because I get to both show and share what's possible for anyone out there impacted by addiction. Recovery is possible, healing and restoring the most important relationships in your life is possible and it's possible for your story to continue with hope, healing and recovery instead of ending in addiction and inevitably death.

The healing that I have done up to this point allows me to see this as an opportunity for continued healing, an opportunity to show up, an opportunity to be of service and to be a part of something really special, sacred, and impactful.

This book is and has been an opportunity and source of healing for my sister, me, and the rest of our family, and that's a beautiful byprod-uct of this work that my sister did, but it wasn't necessarily the focus or the motive. The healing, growth, and love that came out of this project was an extra bonus. My sister felt called to share her experience of how addiction impacted our lives because she knew that it could be the life raft for someone who is currently in the same heart-breaking and hopeless place that she was in, that we were in three years ago. This book is for those whose lives are being touched and turned upside down by addiction right now. This book will speak to those of you who are walking through your own addiction or walking alongside your loved ones struggling with addiction. Through hearing the stories of others, you will find strength and solidarity. You will find allyship, help, and a glimmer of hope.

You will find what you need on the following pages. You need com-munity, and you have it here. You need hope, and you'll find it here. You need to hear someone else say the words that are on the tip of your tongue. You'll find that here, with my sister guiding you through her own story, that it might sound eerily similar to yours.

I know that in these pages you will find what you're seeking. Whether you are an individual in recovery who is working on healing through your own addiction, whether you are currently in addiction seeking to understand your family better, or whether you are a friend, family, or other loved one of an addict who wants to make sure you aren't crazy. You want to hear that your experience is shared. You want to hear in these pages that there is hope. You need a reminder that this seemingly endless rollercoaster of madness that we call addiction can end so that recovery and healing can begin.

I'm so proud of my sister for being able to step up to say the hard shit and share the tough story. Because God knows it's not easy to wade back through the muck, the ick and the mess of emotions that come forward in the recalling of the painful times you have experienced or are experiencing. In whatever way your life has been touched by addiction, it's difficult to trudge back through the memories, pain, experiences to be able to heal through it all and tell the story. My big sister faced this daunting challenge head on and has created something that will undoubtedly be a beacon of light and hope to someone in the middle of their own personal storm.

I am honored to write this prologue. I'm honored to say that without a doubt, you will find support and hope here. You will find a community here even if none of us ever meet. We've got your back. I've got your back. And I know my sister has your back because she has had mine even when I tried to convince her that I didn't deserve it.

Enjoy loving life!

Kaylen

Introduction

LIKE BRAMBLE IN A FINELY CULTIVATED GARDEN, addiction took root in my family. I had no idea or experience of how to be, live or exist with addiction, let alone the heroin, meth and opiate pill-popping **addict** that had become my younger sister. You see, I'm a lawyer, wife, daughter, soul-sister-girlfriend kind of person that lived a predominantly hockey mom life. My younger sister and I were brought up Catholic in the beautiful purity and wild rawness of Alaska. My limited exposure to addiction consisted of my work as a personal injury lawyer, when I represented people that self-medicated with alcohol or opiates. Those infrequent client experiences made an impression and prompted me to volunteer on the Lawyer's Assistance Committee of the Alaska Bar Association, where I was introduced to the misuse of substances by legal professionals as a hack to manage the pressures of a harrowing high stakes law career.

The limited contact I had with drugs and addiction poised me to objectify drug dependency with well-meaning attempts to manage and control my sister with structure, as I would a client in my law office or when I parented toddlers. I created a schedule and blocked time to focus on what appeared to be the core of the chaotic crisis that swirled about me. I developed a research strategy and created an outline of strong and weak points in an attempt to contain the conundrum of this vicious vex that infiltrated our family. I thoughtfully analyzed areas to neutralize and set out bullet points of who was at fault, why and what factors contributed to addiction. The objective was to understand this new and unfamiliar adversary and the aim was to enervate the demon that possessed my sister.

I researched causes of addiction and concluded that none of the usual suspects fit. Our parents weren't alcoholics or addicts. We didn't have a drunken uncle in the family and our childhood was stable, supportive and non-traumatic. We were raised to be active in school events, involved in the community, and attend church weekly. Like our parents, my sister and I had solid educations with advanced degrees. People with stable families do not normally succumb to addiction, or so I thought.

Not finding a familiar origin, I switched gears and approached addiction as a medical condition, similar to when my dad had a heart attack and underwent quintuple bypass surgery, or when the doctors diagnosed my father-in-law with a lung condition or when my uncle and aunties received cancer diagnoses and valiantly stepped into those battles. I figured that equivalent medical protocols for these medical conditions that occurred in our family similarly applied to addiction. I searched for books written by experts in the field of addiction with the mindset that I couldn't be the only human on this planet to encounter addiction. Someone must have a proven approach or protocol to this disorder. There has got to be somebody with initials after their name that has addressed addiction and developed a "best practices guide" to navigate the waters that storm fronted our family. There at least had to be a cliff note version to study up on addiction or some sort of "Addiction for Dummies" with a do it yourself matrix I could implement.

I bought several books, a few with helpful resources about the brain on drugs, but most of the reading material on addiction were sad memoirs of heartbroken family members and washed up, dried out rock stars. I felt that time was not on my side and I simply did not have the emotional bandwidth to absorb these personal accounts. I needed something different and I needed it immediately. I turned to the internet with the thought that in the information age we lived in, a computer search would supply readily accessible answers at my fingertips to a trove of resources. I thought all I had to do was plug in my sister's drug of choice, enter our zip code and my internet search of options and resources would appear on the computer screen. I figured there'd be links to community resource centers with calendars of speakers, events and podcasts on addiction that were educational and informative. What did appear were websites for rehab facilities, twelve step programs, and support groups. I listened to TED talks, watched videos and accessed as much information about addiction that my eyes, ears and brain could absorb. I foraged for and through countless hardcovers and paperbacks, pamphlets, leaflets, went to solemn community events, and talked to people with and without initials after their names with hopes of locating a source of information, or at least a template to overlay onto this toxic paradox that invaded our family.

I spoke with friends and family that could listen; counselors, professional colleagues and anyone that would listen, cared about, loved someone or had a brush with addiction. I met with a medium, mystic, prayed on my knees to patron saints of lost causes and addiction in churches all over the state of Alaska and throughout the lower forty-eight. I reached out to any human on planet Earth who would listen, and reached into the spiritual realm in an effort to clear the air of the tempest cloud of drug dependency that reigned over my sister.

I was unable to find a satisfactory book, solid expert, coach, or guru that could point me in a direction to implement an effective offensive on this goon that squatted and wreaked havoc within our family. I was mystified that in the efficient and streamlined century, country, and world that we lived in, a solution to addiction had not been found. There was not a proven protocol, perfected playbook, magical rubric, streamlined study guide, or cheat sheet checklist to follow and overlay addiction.

So, what's a girl to do that loves an addict and can't find a powerful fount source to eradicate an evil anathema like addiction? All that she can do within her being, and that is what this book is about. These writings recap experiences with my younger sister while in the grips of active addiction. It is a personal perspective of her chronic use of substances that insidiously evolved into severe substance abuse disorder and recounts our hodge-podge resilience over the disease of addiction. This book shares our families' introduction to the disease of addiction, our novice and professional interventions, and the rocky road to treatment, rehabilitation, and recovery with stories of our family's perseverance and survival. This book shares powerful experiences that brought me to the gates of Hell to retrieve my sister and to a grateful bended knee for the evolved supernova kin connection with her that I prayed for. I chronicle traumatic trips and despairing depths that adjusted us from life's normal course to weather and withstand the cold, harsh storm fronts that pummeled our presence, but not our potential.

This book is roller-coaster real and chronicles our family's saga through the years my sister was in active addiction, with portrayals of mishmash systems we devised. I share progressive plays we made against the antagonist that, at times, overwhelmed us. I share tips and tools that worked for me. We colored outside the box during matriculation of the independent study program offered by addiction's school of hard knocks. In the back of this book is an appendix of resources and glossary of bold words with defined terms and concepts that were of support in this journey.

Our family's experience of a drug-directed detour from life's happy highway to passengers on a rickety railway car on Mr. Toads Wild Ride changed how we showed up to play with a faithful energy that transformed our game. Fasten your seatbelt and hold on as the stories go to the deep underbelly of family truths and climb light-headedly high to explore whatever woo-woo would work. Ultimately, and seemingly super naturally, faith, hope, and an exosphere level of love was restored.

This book contains real life stories of what happened to me and everything between me—the mountains, molehills, husbands, parents, children, fur-babies, aunties, uncles, cousins, soul sisters, "**framily**", what I call friends that are family, community—and my sister. To be clear, this book and the words herein will not save you or your loved one, and I am not an expert on the toxic plague of addiction. I'm just a middle-aged woman who walked this road and knows what fit for me, and I offer it to you, the reader, with the hope, love, and faith that pulled me and my family through the chaotic, crazy time warp that addiction is. As is said, take what helps and leave behind what doesn't fit. I am grateful to have the love and blessing of my family, including my sister, to tell these stories with the intention to open hearts, minds, and souls. For it is only with open hearts, minds, and souls that we can love an addict.

1
How Did This Happen?

"HOW DID THIS HAPPEN?" was posed by friends and repeatedly by my mom tearfully when it was just the two of us. To this day I continue to pause when this question is presented. I ground my feet, release my shoulders, and exhale into this complex share. There isn't a Twitter feed response to this curious, well-intentioned ask. There wasn't one thing, a singular moment in time, an event or line that was crossed to summarily showcase how or why "this" happened. At first, it was easy to blame "this" on the man my sister married, and some family members still do. For a while I put the blame on my parents for raising an entitled millennial brat. I felt their over-support of my sister and neglect to instill basic adult life skills to live within one's means, pay bills, save and plan for the future was a fundamental fail on their part. My sister's financial needs were satisfied well past graduate school and into her mid-thirties with my parents' supply of cars, paid deposits, rent, medical expenses, groceries, cell phones, gym memberships, and co-signed contracts.

I also faulted my mom due to the intense, 'push-me-pull-you' bi-polar co-dependent mother-daughter relationship with my sister. My sister and mother's bond volleyed between harsh verbal exchanges to apologetic overcompensations laced with undercurrents of guilt-ridden conditional love. I arraigned and indicted myself for all the **enabling** moments I had with my sister, which included the countless times I bit my tongue and failed to hold my sister accountable for shitty behavior whether it landed on me or our mom. There were the times she stood me up for sister dates, blew off her niece and nephews' school and athletic events, and the occasions she showed up two and three hours late, if at all, to family birthday, holiday or just because gatherings in a self-absorbed dither with lame excuses of what contributed to her delay or absence. There were also all the crisis events in which I rescued her. Thoughtless, careless, and reckless antics while in college, graduate school, and as an emerging adult and into her thirties.

While I'm well aware that my sister was neither holy nor angelic, I hesitate to blame her, though some within our family and community do. They hold the belief that at some point she made the decision to take the toke, swallow the pill, and stick the needle in her arm, and I don't disagree with that point. She did put the needle in her arm. However, I feel that there was something before the needle moment that silently compounded and secretly evolved right under our noses. The "her choice, her decision" proponents expand their anchored reasoning with subjective assertions that there was always a reckless stripe or leaning in her, like that naughty character in *Gremlins*. That discussion is a hard stop for me, as there is no scientific basis to support opinionated character/personality assassinations and it is a waste of precious loving energy to argue with another's narrow noodle of opinionated truth on how "this" happened. The undeniable truth within my knowing is that my sister is a sweet, fierce, scrappy, quirky, loyal, and spirited soul. She will always remain loveable to those that choose and decide to love her.

Last of the suspects is the medical community; including the sugar daddy pharmaceutical industry that in the nineties got a generation of kids hooked and dependent on drugs. I had seen this during the course of my day job when I was a baby personal injury lawyer and witnessed clients and colleagues fall into drug dependency. However, I had no experience or understanding of the medical community's doping of kids to manage childish behavior in a learning environment. This was a cultural medical shift across the nation that my sister had no choice but to get caught up in, lose her footing, and be swept away and lost in that wave of thinking.

When my sister's **active addiction** reached delirium levels, I re-treated to the recesses of my heart, mind, and spirit to till thirty-five years of personal and collective family history as a way to recount how "this" happened. Where was I when "*this*" was happening? Where was mom? Where was dad? What were we all doing? Like the lead character in that *Christmas Vacation* movie that got stuck in the attic, relegated to watch old family films, my mind's-eye recounted scenes from our childhood and growing up years. I searched for a moment in time that the look in her eyes or how she held herself changed. I listened to my parents' wavering memories and weary stories of "raising your sister." I reviewed family photos to discern points in time where she morphed from the little girl that went outside in a snow storm wearing her red lady bug boots to search for our family dog, to the impulsive tattoo and another body piercing, getting edgy Alaskan girl, to a possessed bipolar **junkie** that toggled between shame and rage holed up in a pay-by-the-hour no tell motel. My rational and analytical mind read medical records and searched for mile post signs to retrace our family's steps from turns we missed to map out how my sister got so sick and destitute to piece together her metamorphosis into a homeless heroin addict.

Around the pre-teen time frame, the medical community assessed my sister's excessive talking, restlessness, and impulsivity as Attention Deficit Hyperactivity Disorder (**ADHD**) and recommended that the "knotty" behavior be managed with medication. The next memory I attribute as a major contributing factor to my sister's dependence on substances was when she broke her ankle at the 1998 Arctic Winter games. At the age of fifteen, my sister qualified for Alaska's speed skating team to participate in the international winter sports competition in Canada. At a practice round, she lost an edge on her skate and slid, feet-first, into the rink boards at "break-ankle" speed. In those days, the medical providers thought nothing of supplying a teenager with morphine and other high-level pain relievers to address the agony that broken joint bones generate.

At a young age, my sister's mind and body learned to rely on external substances to manage life's pain and cope with stressors. With the dye cast in her formative brain and body developmental years with physician approved drug-dependent foundation, combined with a diagnosed co-existing brain disorder, my sister ran toward countless, seemingly exhilarating (to her) mind-altering and incautious endeavors.

In high school my sister was social, well adjusted, had a good group of friends, and an age appropriate fine young boyfriend. Being raised in a small community, all the parents knew each other. My sister was (and still is) charming, funny, and strikingly beautiful. Without effort (except for chemistry), she maintained above C average grades and was a strong competitor and leader in any sport, group, or team she participated. My sister's ability to function at a high level through high school with above average grades and athletic abilities allowed the alcohol, mushrooms, pot, and other toxins she consumed to occur under the radar of our parents, coaches, friends, and community.

After high school, my sister matriculated to college as an athlete. Like in her high school years she was high functioning. She's well read, a charismatic conversationalist, physically fit, and an intense competitive college athlete with a compassionate soft spot for the disenfranchised of all sorts, but most especially animals. She was captain of the women's soccer team, as was the man she eventually married from the men's college soccer team. My sister is easy to fall in love with as she's a realist with inspiring optimism and an original sense of humor who is unabashedly loyal to her friends and cohorts. Did I mention that she's gorgeous?

In college, she tried nearly every drug, in addition to the medication prescribed for ADHD and pain from various sporting injuries that included a knee surgery and other muscle wears and tears. The non-prescribed drug use occurred without our knowledge, as my sister exhibited no signs of dysfunction or distress. Indeed, she was successfully playing soccer at the college level with above-average grades and dating the captain of the men's soccer team. After college graduation, my sister entertained the idea of playing women's soccer at a professional level. She chose the education route instead, and attended graduate school for a master's degree in counseling. After completion of her higher education, she obtained a license to practice as a mental health counselor and returned to Alaska to start a practice in her chosen profession. On the outside, my sister looked good and her future bright. She was accomplished, put together, physically fit, and strong; however, on the inside she managed anxiety and frenzied freneticism with extreme reliance and dependency on drugs. We had no idea she was managing life with drugs.

On occasions throughout high school, college, and graduate school, my sister reached out to me with fits of fear and anxiety that I now know were panic attacks. There were extreme mood swings that ranged from paralyzing fear, to audacious impulsivity of bent behaviors, with smatterings of angry outbursts. My mom received the brunt of my sister's rage. An example of my sister's headstrong trait involved a plan to drive across the United States on a spring break road trip with her then college boyfriend and his younger brother while in possession of drugs. While passing through the drug-intolerant state of Texas, the car she was in was stopped by police. My sister and her boyfriend were arrested and jailed. My mom called me in tears. My parents paid to bail her out and for a criminal defense attorney to address this pickle my sister was in that she rationalized as "her Woodstock."

Another contributing factor to my sister's drug dependency was treatment of head and spine injuries she sustained in at least two car crashes, one of which was a roll-over. My sister was the front seat passenger of a car that her husband flipped while driving drunk on a gravel road. She was not wearing a seatbelt (as her dog had chewed through it), allowing my sister's head to impact the interior of the car while in dynamic flipping motion. Indeed, my sister was diagnosed with a concussion and injuries to the discs in the lower spine from that crash. Her ADHD was not re-assessed post-puberty, nor was it re-evaluated in light of the concurring head traumas. She was again supplied opiates to address pain while taking medication to manage ADHD, without indication that the ADHD required continued prescriptive management.

There was legal and medical fallout from the roll-over crash, as her husband was charged with DUI. She was charged with "obstructing justice" for not telling on her husband to the police. However, since her husband left the crash scene to return to the private camp site, our family of attorneys argued that spousal privilege applied and that law enforcement conducted an unreasonable search and seizure of our brother/son-in-law on private property. My husband Chris successfully obtained a dismissal of all criminal charges against our then brother-in-law.

On the medical side of things, my sister was physically injured in the roll-over crash. I was my sister's lawyer in the insurance claim process against the driver of the car, which was her husband, for his negligence in causing her injuries in the roll-over crash. My sister was involved in other car wrecks that aggravated the underlying physical injuries sustained in the rollover crash. More opiate medication was layered on to manage physical pain, all of which was super-imposed over unmanaged ADHD and traumatic brain injury conditions. I successfully pursued several insurance claims on my sister's behalf. Looking back on those times, I'm bothered by how blind I was to her susceptibility to opiate addiction, having practiced in the area for several years. I harbor guilt for my contribution to the protraction of her dependence on drugs by obtaining tens of thousands of dollars on her behalf. With the unmanaged brain diseases coupled with physical pains, being over medicated, with taxed abilities to cope and head trauma's it is no wonder how "this" happened.

My mom's pensive and rhetorical prompt of "how could this have happened" frequently recurred while my sister was in active addiction. Mom's muttered words softly constrained within her delicate chest full of guilt, stigma, and shame. Tears quietly leaked from her big brown eyes and trickled down her pale Irish face. I could see her thoughts dart across her eyes and wash over her with a trundle of traumatic torment within her shrinking body, mind, and spirit. Mom's thoughts of her youngest daughter's addiction were a continuous monkey mind marathon on a feedback loop of recycled anguish that she could not jump off of due to her brain's natural instinct to problem solve. In momma-bear fashion the perceived threat from confabulated notions followed incomplete thoughts to make sense of how this happened. On occasion, mom asked if it was her fault and "does she (my sister) not like us?" It was heartbreaking to be in the presence of our mother's mired hopelessness and despair of how far gone her youngest daughter's condition had become. It is a decision and choice to love others with their varying leanings and that is what got each of us through those dark days and most everything in life.

In those quiet moments that mom and I were alone and she felt safe enough to ask for the umpteenth time, "How could this have happened?" I reassured her that there was no single isolated cause to "this." Kaylen's fall into the hell hole of addiction was not the consequence of a singular bad choice; or the naughty by nature or nurture scenario. It's not a mother's fault, her fault, or my fault; it happened. "This" is multifaceted. It happened and we will get to the other end of it somehow and some way.

My mom's petite five-foot frame and formerly larger than life spirit wearied, and is now withered in part due to the watershed wakes left behind from my sister's self-destructive tidal waves of active addiction. I didn't know it at the time, but my mom's Ph.D-educated, accomplished, problem-solving mind, was diminishing due to her own progressive brain disease. My mom's suffering during the dark days of my sister's active addiction must have been exceptionally horrifying for her. And so I have stopped with the scientific, rationalized theories that lay logical tracks and an accepted off ramp for how this happened. In the end, it just doesn't matter *how* "this" happened. The fact is that it *did* happen. Every family has their story of how "it" happened to them. What matters is how we get through it. I am blessed with the opportunity to share how it happened in our family and how we muddled through one of the most challenging times in our lives, together.

2

How We Learned

IT WAS A LOVELY SUNDAY AFTERNOON, the beginning of the end to a glorious summer weekend filled with doing whatever one wants to do on a timeless Alaskan summer day. My daughter and I were in our respective bedrooms; "being alone together" as my mom used to call it. The July mid-day sun shone steadfast and bright across the green leafed-out valley of trees that sparkled over the distant river and poured into the large, floor to ceiling windows of my bedroom. The windows on each side of the room were open and a soft breeze flowed into the room while the chickadees' signature song and woodpecker taps graced my ears with an organic symphony of surround sound. The dogs and I guiltlessly absorbed this glorious 3D experience, laying on a crisply-made bed airily contemplating "What's next?" while enjoying the fact that whatever is next may be nothing but this.

I relish Sundays as the delightful eclipse between weeks that they are. Sundays are slow awakenings to the potential of a new week; a space in time to absorb the spirituality of the day in a free flow manner and creatively chart out the upcoming week's happenings. There's alone time on Sundays that always feels right, light, fresh, and new. On this Sunday, my attention to immediate family was reduced since my husband and seventeen-year-old son were travelling in the lower forty-eight. There was an added spirit of excitement as the next week was my birthday week.

I sat down in our well-worn sun-faded upholstered chair and placed both legs on the matching ottoman to contemplate the upcoming week. I tend to fast from electronics and social media on Sundays, but this day I felt a pull to catch up on messages from days before. Out of the blue, a high school friend of my sister's sent me a private message on social media:

> Heya! I hope you guys are doing well. Can I have your phone number? We might be out and about and it would be fun to say hi! I love hearing updates from Klen about the kiddos. Sounds like they are amazing. Xox Also, what's your mom's number?

Hmmmmmm, I thought to myself; *a peculiar request.* I was not close with my sister's friends; however, they do all still call me "Sissy" and I was present for a lot of their "moments" that involved my sister, including prom, competitive soccer events, boyfriend break-ups, physical injury recoveries, and my sister's wedding. Also, when raised in a small town it is common to be contacted by family friends, friends of friends, and acquaintances to discuss life situations, especially when your day job is a lawyer. Uncertain of the context of this reach out from my sister's friend, I responded. "Hi there . . . full plate here . . . " and included the requested contact numbers with an apology for the delayed response.

At that time in my life it did feel that there was a lot on my plate. Our family had just adopted two Irish setter puppies, my daughter was studying for a drivers learners permit test, and my son was home from attending school back east for the summer. There was a mediation in a complex sexual harassment and employment discrimination case that I litigated for more than two years scheduled for the upcoming week. Little did I know that this seemingly innocuous reach out from my sister's childhood friend, would be the beginning of the deepest, most intense spiritual hot yoga class that I would ever participate in with my sister.

I prayed for a closer relationship with my sister. I felt my sister was slipping away and didn't know why. I hadn't put the pieces of the puzzle together. Heck, I didn't even know I was working on a puzzle. Over the previous several years, my relationship with my sister had become distant. My sister became withdrawn, aloof, and secluded herself in the clothes-cluttered, dirty-dish mess of an apartment our mom rented for her and her husband. I hadn't seen the loving, loyal, silly, passionate, beautiful, healthy, fierce, carefree Kaylen in a longtime. I noticed this shift when she was in high school. Her disposition had evolved into the person you see at a store that you know you know, but can't quite place well enough to say hi because you don't remember how you know them. I barely recognized my sister anymore. I chalked this expanse between us up to living our adult lives. We were both married, committed to our husbands and doing work in the community as we were raised and educated to do.

The pillars of the person I knew Kaylen to be were crumbling and pieces of our sibling puzzle did not fit. My sister did not make time for our relationship, and rarely if at all directly communicated with me. Tabs on my sister were kept through our mom, who called often with the latest crisis and prayer request for Kaylen and her husband Kyle. After 'the mom call', I would reach out to Kaylen or her husband to invite them out for coffee, a meal, or an event to determine how I could support them through the latest mishap. My sister's top excuses for not meeting up were that she was too sick, had to work, or couldn't afford it.

I responded to her excuses with homemade meals of soup left on her apartment door step. I was never invited into their apartment. I extended invitations to meet up where I pre-paid for everything and waited until she showed up, usually late, if at all. When Kaylen did show up her behavior was rushed, without eye-contact, defensive, and reactionary, like she didn't want to be there. She was pale and bloated. Her jeans and long sleeve hoodies were tight. She gained weight. The hoods on the sweatshirts were over her head or she wore a hat with bright lipstick and eye-brows haphazardly drawn on her face.

I now know the truth behind the excuses. She *was* sick; she was **dope sick**. She *did* have to work because she had fallen so far behind with the paperwork necessary for her employers to maintain their funding. She couldn't afford much of anything because she spent what money she did have on drugs. Her employers reduced her hours, and transferred her patients to edge her out of her job. My sister had become easily overwhelmed and could not hold down a solid paying job in her skill set. The paperwork and professional aspects of the counseling job became too much for her to manage.

My father and I couldn't figure out why she was sick all the time and discussed whether the ADHD diagnosis and head injuries contributed to her inability to meet aspects of her job duties. Kaylen's disorganization, sloppiness, and toggling between anger and panic reached such a point that we contemplated whether she qualified for disability. Anytime I brought those topics up to her, she became defensive and prideful, and accused me of being judgmental. Usually, Kaylen's demeanor with me was receptive; such as when we walked our dogs outside to discuss responses or options to the latest crisis shit-show that surfaced in her life.

When my sister separated from the counseling job, my daughter and I visited her at the locally-owned coffee shop where she worked. By this time, my sister had morphed into a muted, messy, gray, disheveled, and not put-together woman. She acted like a petulant child when she was with her husband. She was mean, bitter, and had a stormy relationship with him. I was embarrassed to be with them as she treated Kyle so poorly with rude intolerant quips and condescending insults. Kaylen and Kyle rarely appeared at family gatherings, and if they did they were hours late and checked out due to the expensive alcohol Kyle drank from a pint glass or the drugs his younger brother did in the back bathroom my sister and I shared in our parents' home. My sister apologized for these happenings, claiming they were one-time events. My husband and I accepted her apology while my father banned Kyle's younger brother from his home.

With me, Kaylen was subdued, shielded, and scattered. She dressed in multiple layers, wore long sleeves and hats that covered her body. Her natural inner beauty was masked and concealed with copious amounts of makeup to hide peeling, splotchy skin and hair loss from her left eyebrow. Her previous long, healthy, luxurious, wavy, dark brown hair was dry, mousy, and positioned to the left side of her face to obscure the changed skin tone and diminishing left eyebrow. When I inquired about her skin tone, complexion, and eyebrow hair loss, she logically and rationally explained it was a dermatological condition that she took medicine for. I now know drug use can increase a hair pulling compulsion to cope with stress and anxiety.*

---

* **Trichotillomania** is a coping strategy for stress, anxiety and obsessive related psychological conditions. Drug use can increase this hair pulling compulsion.

Shortly after I responded to my sister's friend, my mom's number appeared on the caller ID screen of my phone. My chest, heart, and shoulders sank with the thought of another dramatic "mom call." I dreaded mom's calls. It was moms signature M.O. to thickly laid-on Catholic guilt that required the daughter listener to hear a slow reveal of the purpose of her call; usually something about my sister and her latest crisis. It's a weary way to answer the phone and hear the same old pity party story brokered on behalf of my sister. Mom's routine was to call and dump her noxious anxieties about my sister's plights into my earhole. This maternal parental practice started when my sister was a teenager and generally went something like this:

"Michaela, it's your mother. I'm worried about your sister. Please pray for her. She tries so hard. You know (insert sister's time of life here . . . teenagers, athletes, college students, grad students, therapists) don't have a lot of money and she is struggling. I don't think her (teachers, principal, coach, boss) treat her well."

Mom's calls always included content about Kaylen. This time mom's call was different.

> Mom: "Michaela, I just had an unusual experience and need your help."
>
> Me: "What is it mom?"
>
> Mom: "Your sister's friends came to the house, sat in the living room floor of my house and told me that Kaylen does drugs and Kyle gives them to her."
>
> *Silence*
>
> Mom: "Are you there?"
>
> Me: "Yes, I'm here."

Like Dorothy in *The Wizard of Oz*, I felt my being drawn into a cyclone of quandary and confusion as my heart and mind drifted. Mom's panic stricken voice distantly echoed from the phone into the atmosphere like the "Wah, wa, wah, wah's" of adults in a Charlie

Brown cartoon. Mom's voice **moved up** a notch with hysterical "Wah, wa, wah, wah's" that included **words** to the effect of "I don't know what to do! Your father is never here **and I always** have to handle these things myself!" Mom then switched **to paralyzing** fear for my sister's health and how to tell my dad; afraid **he would** blame her for this quagmire.

Unable to process the information and unwilling to accept that her younger daughter was a drug **user**; my mom vacillated between sobs and fits of rage with indignant, rhetorical PhD-type questions about the information left with her **by Kaylen's** friends, who are kind and solid people my parents have **known** since they were pre-teens. That's the thing about mom; when it **comes** to family, especially her younger daughter, if something untoward **was** expressed, then mom framed the expression as fallacy or disloyalty. "Who are they to know, how could they know? Why would they **turn on** her like this?"

I attempted to rationalize **with mom** that Kaylen's friends had no reason to lie or supply incorrect **information**. I offered to help tell dad what Kaylen's friends told her. I **ended** the conversation with my mom and sat with the information I **had just** learned. I didn't know how to feel or what to do. Like lava **surging** and ready to erupt, my emotions swelled and fell upon each other, bubbled to the surface and poured out of me. I attempted to **contain** the feelings to not disquiet my empathically insightful daughter, **who** was upstairs in her room doing what pre-teen girls do.

I closed the door to my **bedroom** to purge the sorrow within my gut, and had a grief stricken sob session. I now recognized and could make sense of various instances of Kaylen's offbeat behaviors. It was like watching an old nostalgic **movie** enjoyed as a kid with greater understanding and appreciation **of the** subtleties by an older self. The always being late or not **showing up** because she was "sick"; her unhealthy and disheveled appearances of scabby and bruised skin; never inviting me into her apartment; the dirty, unkempt apartment; her inability to manage money; not **attending** family gatherings; the rages she laid upon Kyle for anything **and** my mom about money for "her medication"; all the jobs she **lost** and random people staying at the gross apartment and unknown **persons** using cars my parents gave her now made sense.

My mind next darted to all the times my kids were at her apartment and my children's exposure to the drug life Kaylen and Kyle lived. Unable to hold the weight, tears, and emotion alone, I called my husband. He quietly listened and served as an anchor in these choppy deep waters with kind attention and strength to my uncharacteristic expressions of sorrow. We recounted each time our children were with Kaylen and Kyle at the apartment, and decided to inform our children of their auntie's drug use with direction that it was not safe to be near their auntie or uncle.

I now know that the seemingly benign message from Kaylen's childhood friend was the start of a journey that would push me beyond my human control freak limits. The next two years would stretch my rigid, inflexible, type A personality into challenging positions, unfamiliar places, and painful relationship spaces with my sister with an existential force greater than gravity. The next day I messaged my sister's friend: "My mom called and said she met with you . . . that took great strength and courage . . . Thank you."

Her response: "Hey Michaela, I really felt like we had no option. I'm really glad your mom went ahead and talked to you about it now. I didn't want her to be left alone with it. Let me know if you want to talk more."

My sister's friend went on to explain that Kaylen was not the person they knew her to be and relayed that they could tell by looking at her that she was in the "**denying phase.**" Kaylen claimed that the events her friends recounted to our mom were blown out of proportion; that she was fine, had been doing counseling for ten years and knew what was best.

Her friends informed me about "**detox**" facilities that assisted with withdrawals, and organizations that provided "**rehab**" and recovery. All these new words and phrases were from a vocabulary list I had not studied or been exposed to. Like *Alice in Wonderland*, I felt lost in a land I had fallen into; a paradoxical world with a new language that seeped out of the face of a grinning Cheshire cat with its shameless shit-eating grin.

The next several days were spent processing this staggering information. Nothing made sense and I was a-wash with destabilizing, confusing and opposing emotions. I was horrified, angry, ashamed, embarrassed, disappointed, disgusted, scared, sad, and guilt-ridden for not knowing. This tornado of feelings was focused, cycled, and recycled on one person—my sister—who I loved. It's a piercing place to be in the center of a cyclone shit storm centered on a person you love.

I knew nothing about drug addiction, let alone the story of how my sister was caught up and connected with it. I had no idea the depth and breadth of my sister's addiction. Who else knew my sister was an addict while I had been oblivious, seeming distant, and a removed older sister? Did my kids' teenage friends know? Did my brother-in-law deal drugs to my kids' friends? Did my sister's friends, who I also know as friends and clients, know about the drug life my sister and her husband lived? How could I be so daft? How did my sister and I, become so disconnected when we lived in the same small town and knew the same people?

In between the messages and calls from my sister's friends, my mom continued to repeatedly call me several times a day after her rides on the emotional roller coaster that overwhelmed her with **co-dependent** adrenalin rushes. Mom's fretful chronicles to me ranged from yelling rants to contrite tearful apologies and every confusing emotion in between.

Out of one side of my mom's mouth she dumped polarizing nonsensical and ridiculous expressions about my sister "that she does not use every day and I know addicts lie," and out of the other side of her manic matriarchal mouth demanded family loyalty while puzzlingly infusing irrational condescending scorn, "What do her friends know? They're not counselors." My mom's reactions and constant frantic calls were completely unhelpful, confusing, and hurtful, especially when she made accusations of me being disloyal or not caring. I struggled to navigate how to show up with each member of my family, in the community, and to step out of the front door of my life to walk in the brave new world knowing my sister was an addict. I carried these heavy weights in my new back pack of life under dark clouds until dad returned from fishing.

The next couple of days I walked in a post-apocalyptic emotionally and spiritually vacant zombie land. I felt alone and could not make sense of a world I had enjoyed just days before. A dark shadow fell.

When I drove through our quaint community to my parents' house I'd look at shady pockets of neighborhoods and ponder whether Kaylen and Kyle sold drugs there. I'd encounter friends and people I knew at stores or restaurants and question in the back of mind, if they knew.

Mom and I set up the reveal to dad when he returned from fishing. I drove the forty minutes to my parents' house and pondered how to divulge "this" to my father. As I walked into the living room of my parents' house, pounding harsh voices of political commentators blared from a television and reverberated off the walls. My dad lounged comfortably in his light blue fabric covered recliner he bought years ago to convalesce from hip, heart, and knee surgeries. Mom sat next to him perched nervously at the edge of the brown leather tea stained couch and vacantly stared at the television. I recognized mom's facial expressions of panic and unease when I entered the spacious cathedral ceiling family room.

I resumed the place I had sat as a teenager when I lived in that house, cross legged on the cream, cat hair-covered carpeted floor adjacent to dad's recliner and across from mom. Mom's precognitive telepathic anxious eyes locked with mine, and visually pressed me to tell him. My jaws locked and stomach sank as I acknowledged to my adult self that I was to step into the lead on this one. It's a sticky, heavy weight to regulate a reveal to your elder lawyer dad that his younger daughter is a drug addict, especially when the content is based on tales of what my sister's friends said. I inhaled deeply and pensively expressed on the other side of the newspaper he was reading something along the lines of:

"Hey dad, we need to tell you something."

He put the paper down on his lap, moved the recliner to the upright position and looked at me over his taped reading glasses that crookedly hung across his eyes.

"Leia and Wren came to the house and told mom that Kaylen's doing drugs and Kyle supplies them to her. They told us that they know Kaylen is doing drugs because she admitted to it and she has been acting erratically and outside the norm while they've been visiting her here in Alaska."

Silence.

My father did not move and continued to look at me over the broken reading glasses. Slowly he turned to look at mom and instantaneously, vicious verbal combat broke out between my parents. My mom, whose emotions had swelled within her like a bottle of seltzer water, reopened old wounds and stridently accused my dad of not being a supportive co-parent in raising their daughter saying that, "This never would have happened if you hadn't allowed her to live in that **flop house** of an apartment you own when she got married."

My dad defensively turned the conversation to me saying "You see, this is what she does, she blames me."

He then counterattacked that my mom had financially enabled my sister for decades with a constant outlay of cash; paying her bills and giving her cars. He used gas lighting snipes as well, saying that my sister's addiction was the product of a toxically neurotic mother-daughter relationship.

Within moments, the family room where my family had danced, played board games, watched movies, gathered with friends, celebrated birthdays, and holidays for four decades was overtaken by a senseless, bitter poison that exposed itself through my parents go-to, default coping strategies of contemptuous blame and malicious cross examination of each other, while the vile villain of addiction laughed. My heart sank as a new reality hung over my family like a heavy cloak. Addiction 1, Kelleybury's 0.

3

Slow Mo Mobilization

FOR THE FIRST TIME IN MY LIFE, my parents were close lipped about the elephant in the room. They were hopelessly disappointed, grief stricken, and ashamed. They built separate turreted fronts fortified with resentment and went into isolation. My parents became sullen, and insulated themselves; rarely coming out to meet with me or their friends. There was no way they could problem solve. It must have been gut-wrenching for my parents to watch their younger daughter slowly swirl into a nose dive and not be able to extend a safety net for her.

Dad was brusque. He never stepped into Kaylen's latest crisis and was resolute that he would not enable her drug addiction in any way. Dad begrudged mom's financial support of Kaylen and was unwavering. He made a rule that no cash or money can be given to Kaylen. Dad was assured that he didn't do anything to contribute to Kaylen's drug dependency. He'd say, "I know she was raised right." Dad treated Kaylen's addiction like a bad business partner and cauterized exposed loose ends of vehicle titles, insurance policies, and estate matters to protect from the harm that might occur while Kaylen and Kyle were in active addiction.

Local police, friends, and people from the community called with their latest Kaylen or Kyle encounter. They'd say they had to ask Kyle to leave for selling drugs or commented on Kaylen's over-reaction and disheveled appearance. While in this front row seat to Kaylen's descent, dad and I commiserated and noted her slip down another notch to whatever her **rock bottom** might be. *Can it get any lower?* I'd ask myself, not saying out loud that her rock bottom might be death.

Mom resisted accepting her younger daughter's drug dependency. Mom did not talk about Kaylen's life situation with dad, as it usually devolved into a fight. Nor did she speak publicly about Kaylen. Mom internally processed Kaylen's current life situation and called me to deposit her grief, anxiety, and rage. I had to tell mom that I could no longer take these calls and hung up. Mom immediately called back and continued to push whatever issue was on her mind; always Kaylen and now her drug dependency.

Sometimes I'd answer mom's calls, often I didn't. I just couldn't be there and take it; or listen to her anymore. When I did answer the phone out of Catholic daughter guilt, mom would apologize for what she had said and roll right back into grief and depression. Mom's blowing through anger, grief, resentment, and contriteness like toll booths on a superhighway was exhausting for me and had to be hell for her. I contemplated whether mom was emotionally overwhelmed, bipolar or something else; losing her mind maybe. I finally had enough and told her that it was not fair to place her anger at dad, or her ire and grief about Kaylen with me as I loved them both, and her, too.

On the weekends, mom pulled out of her anguish and despair to meet with Kaylen and attempt to singlehandedly fix her addiction. As a trained therapist, mom took it upon herself to reason and **bargain** with Kaylen and supply self-interested counseling. Mom did mini-**interventions** with Kaylen on the doorstep of the apartment with a pseudo delivery of therapy skills. Mom called me after these sessions to report how Kaylen looked and what efforts Kaylen had made to get off drugs. Mom would then fall into a grief-stricken hollowness which quickly elevated to rage, with snide swipes toward me and dad of how she felt alone in this fight to save Kaylen. Mom then moved to soft words of contrition, saying, "She's really trying." She'd then ask me to keep my sister in my prayers and requested that I check on her.

I re-engaged with a counselor that I had seen year's earlier and suggested mom do the same, thinking it would be a nice two-fer for mom to have the same dumping ground rather than using the acreage in my heart and soul as her personal emotional leach field to deposit her fear, grief and anger. At first mom resisted seeing a counselor. I was frustrated and confused when she balked at seeing a counselor, since she was a therapist herself and had seen one in the past. Seeing a counselor was the best thing I ever did. I left all those messy, unfixable, and exhausting emotions over my sister, brother-in-law, parents, spouse, and how to raise my children in this new reality in the therapist's office. I learned to leave it all there. Revealing the truths surrounding Kaylen's addiction was destabilizing. The truth was that Kaylen could not support herself and could not hold down a job.

It was a big ask for my independent minded mom to bear witness to the truth of herself and her younger daughter's current life circumstance and accept that her previous boasts about Kaylen were all fiction in her Catholic Boomer generation mind. Another resistance factor for mom to enter therapy was fear of what was happening to her own brain might be revealed. Mom's rants, unregulated thoughts, and extreme emotional patterns might be something happening to her that existed concurrently with Kaylen's drug dependency. Perhaps mom had just enough rational bandwidth to not want to go there and not want to discover the truth of what was happening within her own brain. Or maybe mom wanted to keep that truth an inside secret for as long as possible, or at least until her daughter was better. The truth was mom was slipping down a drain of her own while Kaylen was tumbling down another, both keeping secrets of their need for help.

A client once said to me, "When you speak words out loud to another person, it makes it real." Feelings spoken out loud in counseling sessions are released truths. Eventually mom honed what I thought was hubris and conjured the courage to meet with a counselor. It was a big step for mom and took great fortitude for her to speak with another in the field she taught, delivered, and mastered as a legacy. Mom's meet ups with "her guy," as we coined it, proved beneficial. Her loyalty rages and grief stricken depression dumps on me lessened. We learned **boundaries** of our own, with each other and began to share "best practices" to maintain our sanity.

I connected with my sister every so often to walk her dog. My sister avoided discussions of her health and drug use. The focus of Kaylen's dialogue consisted of work challenges with her supervisor and co-workers. She blamed her employer of converting clients and edging her out of a job. Kaylen spoke in half-truths. I listened and mentally aligned with her supervisor thinking *I would say and do the same.* Kaylen obliquely shared the next self-created crisis as if she was a victim of circumstance. I learned to listen to what was not being said. Kaylen felt the world was against her and that others were out to get her. Her stories were three steps of what appeared to be legit **recovery** progress, then two giant steps backwards that exposed shallow superficial efforts. It is hard to unconditionally love someone while sorting through their twisted truths while simultaneously holding space for them under the strain of manipulative moves. Kaylen was slipping deeper into addiction right before my eyes and there was nothing I could do.

Kaylen cleaned up well when she connected with me or mom. She posted pretty pictures of herself on social media of hikes and other wellness activities and posted them as proof to the outside world that she was doing well and did not have a drug dependency problem. Behind the scenes and posting of her on top of a mountain with her dog, Kaylen and Kyle were barely holding on. Kyle was fired from every job he got and Kaylen's job as a counselor was at risk as she could not manage paperwork or show up to deliver services. The same late arrival or not appearing at family gatherings continued, but at least there was the courtesy of a text of their delay or cancellation. Sometimes I'd see a glimmer of the real Kaylen; her love of animals or her clutch of a pillow-case I had made special for her. But most of the time, Kaylen's existence and narrative was disheveled murmurs that blamed others for her plight and position in life.

I invited Kaylen to a yoga retreat with the thought we would have some time together to do some healthy self-care that may be good for her and our relationship. I was disappointed and sad when she did not show up to the retreat after having promised that she would. I felt used and lied to. Kaylen and Kyle did make the two-hour drive to my husband's fiftieth birthday at a seaside campsite, albeit late. It was awkward as they stayed at a campsite on the hill away from the family, probably to use drugs. The kids and in-laws had not seen Kaylen and Kyle for several months. There's a part of me that cherishes that camping birthday moment, as it was the first time Kaylen and Kyle engaged with my in-laws. Kaylen and Kyle went on a hike with their niece, nephew, and the dogs that weekend and Kyle caught his first fish. My mother- and father-in-law were so gracious to Kaylen and Kyle that weekend. It was the last time that Kaylen and Kyle saw my father-in-law before he died that following winter, succumbing to a lung disease. They did not attend my father-in-law's memorial service.

I went into planner/fixer mode and reached out to peers and colleagues familiar with addiction in search of resources, support and options to address what was happening. I reached out to a colleague who sat on the **Lawyer's Assistance Committee** with me that had personal experience with addiction. He graciously took my call and compassionately listened to the story about my sister. Like a priest in a confessional, he heard about all the times I took care of, rescued, saved, and advocated for my sister. He gently commented, "The things we do to help the people we love." With comforting words of understanding, he honored the love our family had for Kaylen and noted that each of us were in "helping professions." He pointed out that it is in our very nature to implement a "fix it" response to those we love. I felt like I had found an ally. His words and observations made me feel better about myself and who I was in that moment in time. His words exposed the raw **codependent enabling** nerve root at the base of our family tree.

My colleague went on to share a story of his drug addicted adult son that he drove to a homeless shelter to wearily tell his son that he had to stay here. When my friend shared his story with me, I felt for the first time that I was not alone in this world. I was not the only one that loved an addict. Eventually, my friend's son found recovery, became employed and stayed clear of drugs. My friends experience cast a beam of hopeful light on the dark and foreign trail I was travelling. We ended our conversation with his sharing the name and number of some help lines, and that was what introduced me to John, an **interventionist**.

That next week, I called the number my friend had given me from the safety and privacy of my car in a Walmart parking lot. I hesitated before I dialed the numbers and contemplated, *how do I initiate a conversation with a complete stranger on the topic of my sister's drug addiction? Fuck it, just do it, Michaela.* And so I dialed the number. A man with a kind voice answered the phone. With my game face on and emotions contained, I introduced myself as proficiently as I could and relayed the heavy narrative of our family's plight to him. He listened to my tale and then suggested a combined intervention for Kaylen and her husband Kyle.

I knew a joint intervention was a hard stop for my dad. Dad made it clear that he would not participate in an intervention that included Kyle, or as my dad referred to him, "the man that married his younger daughter." My dad felt that Kyle was irresponsible and that he did not live up to the commitment he had made to Kaylen and significantly contributed to her drug dependency. I explained to John that there were control issues in Kaylen and Kyle's marriage that may reframe good intentions of a joint intervention into a dramatic shit show about their relationship instead of Kaylen's rehabilitation. I shared that family and friends harbored resentment towards Kyle and were not in a place to separate the hard feelings they had for Kyle from the unconditional love they have for Kaylen.

By no means was this to sound scape-goaty. We all knew very well that Kaylen, our sister, daughter, auntie, and friend, was no angel, nor was she free of blame for what had become of her life. Nevertheless, the dysfunctional marriage relationship was a significant contributing factor and concurrent condition that would distract from any attempt at Kaylen's rehabilitation, and at that time, our family's emotional capabilities were limited. We were simply unable to expand our efforts to include one to two additional addicts of Kyle and his younger brother. It would be too much.

As promised, John sent the materials that explained what an intervention was and how it is done. The materials arrived at my business address in large yellow manila envelope marked personal and contained a seventies style educational VHS tape with his cards, resume and literature on addiction. It was auspicious that nearly twenty years into a new millennium a VHS tape was sent to a family that still had VHS players. I placed the materials in my bag to watch in the privacy of my home.

Once home, I unwrapped the materials from the envelope and with my left brain tendencies fuddled with the home entertainment electronic system my husband had installed in our living room while he prepared our dinner in the kitchen. I switched the input/output HDMI thingies to the correct settings, sat down at the wooden dining table and maneuvered the stiff dining room chair for a front seat view. I pushed the play button on the remote control and watched the video alone.

A somber screen showed people as dated as the VHS tape, with content by addiction specialists that explained addiction as a disease that called for an equivalent approach one would provide to a friend or family member that had suffered from a heart attack. What I saw on the video made sense to me. The video explained what an intervention was, why it is done, and how it is done. The video explained science-based interventions for those medical conditions and, similarly, interventions for the addiction illness that our loved one suffered from. *Finally*, I thought, *someone gets it!* I felt validated in my emotional state and approach to Kaylen's addiction.

I watched the video again with my husband as we ate dinner. I watched the video a couple more times to get it fully into my system. At the following Sunday coffee with my parents, I gave the intervention materials and video to them. For several more months they remained stuck in a glue trap of shame, disappointment, sadness, and anger that made them incapable of opening the manila envelope of materials John sent. I'd see the crumpled envelope tucked out of reach and direct sight at the top of the book shelf at their house. When I asked my parents about the video and materials, dad would snap that he didn't want to put his time or focus there. "Kaylen should be doing the research herself," he'd say. Mom questioned everyone's qualifications to disseminate information on interventions. These responses perplexed me since dad previously participated in an intervention for an alcoholic friend and mom found support with groups and therapy when her close friends died.

Several months passed before my parents stopped blaming each other and whoever or whatever was at fault for Kaylen's drug dependency. Nearly half a year went by before my parents opened up beyond the confines of themselves, each other, and me. It was like beginning weight training class for them to garner strength and gain understanding about substance dependency, how it evolved into abuse with Kaylen, and admit the sad truth of her dependence on drugs to friends, neighbors, and the community. By the time my parents' fiftieth wedding anniversary celebration came around, mom was able to craft a deliverable response to the well-intentioned ask of, "How are you and how's Kaylen?" Mom would say: 'I'm sad. My younger daughter Kaylen is sick and when I talk about it I start to cry." Friends and neighbors graciously responded with, "Okay, then we won't talk about it," and they moved onto another topic.

As we each stepped onto the trail of understanding and acceptance of Kaylen's substance abuse disorder, time marched on, the distance from Kaylen grew, her **substance use disorder** persisted, grew, and her world continued to devolve and destabilize while addiction continued to gain ground.

4

Across the River

MY HEART WAS OUTSIDE MY BODY, bleeding for all to see. I've never been good at hiding my emotions. I wear them on the outside of my body with a flushed face and red splotches on the fair skin of my neck and chest like a chemical burn. Thank goodness I live in Alaska so I can dress in layers; to cover up and hide the overt distress signals that automatically ensue from my body. While my sister slid uncontrollably down a double black diamond slope to the hell hole of nowhere, I retracted deep inside myself. It took great effort for me to maintain a vacant straight face as I walked spiritless through another day of life. It felt like I was living a lie. I pretended to be present and focus at my day job. I no longer wore make-up. Why? I'd just cry it all off and I hate asking others if my mascara is smeared. It comes across as so needy.

I kept to myself; I shut my mouth, locked my jaw, clasped my teeth, and swallowed the poison pill of unexpressed sentiment that welled inside of me. I sealed myself off from the world with lonely, desolate thoughts of Kaylen and her addicted lifestyle. Tears of mental exhaustion flushed out of me at unexpected moments. Everything was a **trigger**. That crooning song by Harry Styles inevitably streamed out of the radio that told me to stop crying. *Well Harry, I can't stop crying right now and quit telling me what to do!* At our town's sole intersection traffic light my face was a puddled mess of full on waterworks. *Don't turn your head. You probably know the other drivers and they'll see you crying. They're probably your kids' friends and they'll say 'Hey, saw your mom at the stop light she was crying. Is she okay?' And then my kids would* *have to talk about how sad I am that my sister, their auntie, is a drug addict. Thanks a lot, Harry.* Harry sang directly to me. It became an indicator to me that my angels were close.

I tried to pray. I was never taught how to pray, so I prayed to what I thought were my angels. I prayed to whoever and whatever I thought would help or listen. I pray cried in my car with Harry in the background to the dead grandfather I had never met, thinking he was my sister's grandfather too, maybe he could help. I pray cried to the grandfather I knew well and to our grandmother that married both of those men. I also pray cried to my grandmother's first daughter, my auntie who was my sister's godmother. My thinking was that our auntie-godmother could get together with my dead grandparents, present the matter to 'the big guy' as she used to call him and pull some miraculous intervention.

I separated myself from community spaces. I attended church and shopped for groceries in the next town over to avoid encounters with people I knew. I didn't want to engage in the inevitable asks of, "How are you? How are the kids? How are your parents?" Truthful response to these kinds of well-intentioned verbal preludes sat in a straight jacket at the hinge of my jaw behind clinched teeth with fake smile. If my unhinged jaw could talk, it would say *I'm not well. I'm not well at all. All hell is breaking loose in my life right now. The kid's auntie, my sister, is an IV drug user. I'm always crying. I'm not present for my kids and my husband doesn't know how to support me in this shit show of a mess. My mom is beside herself with despairing grief and my dad is decidedly disappointed, and that's an understatement. I don't like seeing my parents anymore. I don't even want to see you right now. I'm embarrassed by my sister and it's a total humiliating, depressing drag that my sister is a junkie-ass loser."*

But I couldn't say that out loud in public to people that I have known for over forty years. These seemingly mundane and previously enjoyable questions disquietedly settled into a weighted blanket over my shoulders and a twisted dagger in the gaping open wound of my heart.

I hated the phone and dreaded all of the sounds and lights that come from it. Phone sounds startled me. A ring from a phone sent anxious thoughts through a mental rolodex of potential callers. *Was it a call from the jail with that faraway sounding pre-recorded audio to accept a call from an inmate? Was it a first responder or junkie with a heart calling that she died of an overdose?* I held my breath when the phones dinged until I knew who was calling and why. I panicked when calls from unknown numbers appeared on my phone. *What junkie,* **kingpin, trafficker** *has her phone and now my number to extort, exploit or harm her, me or my family?*

Police notifications, texts of forwarded data from well-intentioned friends of encounters with Kaylen and her raw social media posts pummeled me like George Foreman punches. At the same time, I wanted to see posts of my sister's destruction to confirm where she was and that she was still alive, even if it was barely. I checked the time of posts and enlarged pictures to the pixels for clues about her health, well-being and location.

I resented the fact that control of my day shifted to demons that ran at night and set a neurotic tone for the ensuing days that had no end or beginning. Time, day, and night were a long marathon continuum. I felt that I was in some kind of fucked up ground hog day. I wanted out of the game and out of the movie. I missed my mornings. I missed my peace and I wanted it back. I wanted my days back. I wanted my time back. I wanted my life back. I was tired of the relentless thumping by whomever or whatever was on the other end of the phone.

I went across the river to the next town to quietly cry, wander aisles, sit by myself, pray, and sort the nonsensical without interruptions by well-meaning others. I refrained from revealing to good-intentioned people the cataclysmic cloud of jihad chaos behind door number one of my heart that initiated a hostile takeover of my sister. I didn't want to turn into a crying mess in the dairy aisle and make things weird with a fellow hockey mom. It was not necessary for me to release my sad truth onto others. So, as a way to cope, I placed our family's lack of well-being on the far side of the discussion table, next to the pistachio pudding and cranberry sauce that everyone overlooks.

I walked with my wilted spirit in the safe and distant space across the river. I was detached from encounters with true blue neighbors that could see something was off with me. My remote wanderings allowed my disassociated presence to hear the sweet high pitched truth of a child's voice that asked, "Why is the lady crying?"

The gentle wind of the grown up response of, "I don't know, she must be sad," swept over me like the blessing that it was on a heavy day. It feels so good to wordlessly go away and release the weighty spiritual luggage onto the trees for their branches to lift up to the clouds and into the wind to evaporate and waft into the atmosphere and rain down someplace else further down as a beautifully repurposed, new-to-them cleansed truth.

I made a list of what made me happy and what was good for me. I started with the basics and took baby steps. I began with hydration. I like water and water is good for me. Each happy and good for me thing I jotted down and made into a superior moment, like a mother does for her child's birthday to squeeze every ounce of goodness from that activity since things in the outside world were so shitty. So I upped the game to lemon water and included walking in nature and my dogs to the list of things that I like and are good for me

I prepared for my morning well-being time (**MWBT**) each night with a routine that conditioned my mind and body to wind down. I pre-poured myself a glass of lemon water and placed it on the nightstand beside my bed so it was ready first thing in the morning. I figured that it was a good for me life hack to start the day with a clean palate. Sleep is another thing that I like, makes me happy and is good for me. I made a spot for the phone and charger away from my bed and set do not disturb hours. I reviewed each day, and counted all the blessings and wins throughout the day as a gratitude practice. I wound down the day and laid out the essence of the next day starting with MWBT. I aimed for seven hours of sleep and back-tracked time blocks from there to select a wake time and MWBT. This evening routine laid the grounding track to pull the shade at the end of each day and open a curtain to the next. No longer would I run a never-ending forever marathon on a treadmill I didn't know how to stop or hop off of.

I prepared for MWBT like I would for time with a loved one. I fashioned a comfortable spot for me to be with a candle, journal, pen, and timer. I woke the next morning, drank the lemon water, and moseyed to the kitchen to make myself the best cup of coffee ever; another thing that makes me happy. I did morning stretches with my dog that made me happy and felt good. I let the dog out to do his thing and observed with gratitude the surroundings of a quiet morning; the cold deck on my feet, the glow of the moon off the snow, and sometimes the extra blessing of a hooting owl. I next moved to my meditation station, aka MWBT, to light the candle, set the timer, and focus on an area that needed more light. For me a timer is necessary to audibly close MWBT. I have a tendency to get lost in my head with circular thoughts. If there was extra time, I read thoughtful passages, articles, or books recommended by friends.

MWBT starts with the breath. Breathe in what is wanted, what you feel you need and want to bring into your life. Exhale what others and the universe need. For me, this was a breath cycle of inhaling peace and exhaling love. In the wee-hours of MWBT, I prayed for Kaylen and a connection to her. I wrote in my journal. When the timer chimed, the MWBT session stopped. Some mornings were five minutes, others were twenty or more. It's amazing how effective a two minute breath cycle feels. I ended my MWBT with gratitude and writing down three things I was grateful for. I wrapped up MWBT with a large inhale and blew out the candle with my exhale that sent peaceful wishes for the day out to others within the universe.

I noted whether there was a full plate day ahead of me and planned mini well-being sessions to transition between big moments. A two minute wellness session in my car to find the breath and return to myself, who I am in the moment, and how I show up is so worthwhile. When intrusive thoughts knocked on the door of my mind through-out the day as the dinging distractions that they are, I acknowledged the existence of those gnats and that we'd discuss this further at the next appointed time.

Pre-dawn MWBT quieted my mind, salved my heart, opened my soul, and lifted my spirit. I conditioned my mind to go where I want-ed it to go and focus on what I wanted to focus on. MWBT supplied re-entry space to discern how I would show up for the day and laid a solid foundation for how I stood in times of uncertainty. I visualized how I walked through the day and discerned every potential "what if." I walked my mind through daily grind concerns of how to get through a deposition without crying, how to show up at a social event and respond to the inevitable 'how's your sister' question, and muddle my way through the tearful truth of addiction in our family.

I journaled how I wanted to handle these situations rather than allow my reactionary emotions dictate the day. I reflected on how to love and support the people in my life, especially my sister, with all the harm she was doing to herself and the ripple effects on others. I pondered public postings of Kaylen's latest exploits and reflected on what I would do, if anything, when Kaylen called or texted. I meditated on the counteractive convictions of not knowing if I could trust Kaylen and the fact that I loved her at the same time. I contemplated the moment a stranger might reach out to me about Kaylen's well-being.

MWBT enabled me to connect with who I was and how to step into destabilizing moments. My father always said to do what you don't want to do first, that way it's done, over with, and you can go on to the other stuff with ease. So, in MWBT I contemplated the big stuff. I visualized what I feared the most: death by overdose and Kaylen's funeral. I imagined receiving a call from my parents that Kaylen had died and her memorial service. I wrote Kaylen's obituary and eulogy because I knew I would have to do it anyway, so I might as well do it then. I read them both out loud in the mirror so that I was no longer afraid of the worst thing that could happen. I knew the likelihood that these moments could surface was high. I wanted dominion over that potentiality rather than a life of living in and hiding from fear of it happening. I was so done and exhausted with fear controlling me. I wanted to be grounded in who I was in whatever moment came my way and how I showed up. I knew that no matter what, I would always show up in truth and love.

Mornings were, and still are, a solitary oasis of self-awareness to examine my role in the flow and chaos of life. I'm able to drill down on what I want to do, what I am capable of doing and what limitations exist. To truthfully know where, why, and what I am called to do. Hopeful intentions, thoughtful objectives and faithful mindsets align in MWBT. MWBT is how I arrived at the mantra to hope and pray for the best, prepare for the worst, and that reality usually falls somewhere in between.

I incorporated walking outside into my well-being plan, as it is another thing that makes me happy and is good for me. I'm blessed that I can walk in the woods that surround my house. Walks in nature soothe me. When my sister was in active addiction, tears over her untethered soul flowed out of me and into the earth as an organic cleanse that served to ground me. Walking in nature as a part of my daily routine is now non-negotiable for me. My walking goal is at least 30 minutes a day. If I feel chained to the desk, I set the timer on the hour for a five to ten minute walk. On a full plate day, I break walks down to occur throughout the day, every hour, even if it's six, five-minute walks.

I acquainted myself with unfamiliar feelings that I had locked away for whatever reason; perhaps because I thought they were too emotional, a waste of time, unproductive or too much. I call these red flag feelings (**RFF**). When RFFs reached a fever pitch, I made time for them and did what I felt was needed, just like I would with a close friend. Sometimes I made a cup of tea for my wilted spirit, like I would a sad grieving friend. This practice allowed hard feelings of guilt and irresponsibility for the disassociated presence that occupied me to exist. Other times I took my angry, condescending bitch-ass self on a walk to release the resentful recounts that my sad sop of a lost self was a waste of time, space, and energy, and that the heavy hopeless ocean of tears were a worthless waste of time and weak emotional energy. I gained friendship with the RFFs within me. No longer was I afraid of experiencing those challenging emotions. The time and space that I made for RFFs allowed for my arrival at peace. I gained a new and improved brand of strength to hold the line with the desolate truths of all the hard feelings that surround and abut addiction.

Pro tip for those that love people that love addicts, all you can do is stand with, hold space for, and listen to the person you care about that is suffering. Hugs are nice too, and don't let go until it feels right. There are no good words or deeds to offer at the threshold of that conversation portal to the desolate, unknown space your loved one occupies. You cannot make things better and they know that. Just be real and love on them to your capacity, your way. Assure them that they're seen, that their tears are okay, and that you are there for them.

Several months passed until I came to terms with the stigma and humiliation of my sister's status and accepted that she was sick and needed help. I arrived at a place that there is no control and no out-thinking addiction. You just have to be with it. There is no linear map of where a loved one's addiction will go. Addiction marches on, gathering minion pawns, and counting bodies. The key is to know how to be with it and how you will show up when it is present and at the door.

5

Trip of a Lifetime

MY DAD PLANNED A TRIP OUT OF THE COUNTRY. Not a one to two week trip to Cabo or Hawaii, but a once in a life time trip he designed for over a year to another country to see big animals he had not seen in Alaska. Dad couldn't wait to get out of the frigid state of Alaska and leave all of the crap of Kaylen and Kyle in the frozen lands behind him. I held onto the hopeful thought that my parents would have space and time to be with each other, really be with each other and see things together that made them happy. Like a kid of separated parents, I wished the time they had together, away from the rinse, wash, repeat crisis d'jour cycles of Kaylen's addiction would draw them closer together without constant reminders of the current circumstances of their youngest daughter's addiction and homelessness. With the right amount of space my parents might be able to reframe and focus on connecting, healing, and being with each other rather than the constant re-prick of resentment scabs they held for each other that each felt contributed to Kaylen's demise.

Dad requested that a family church friend check on the house, plants, and animals while they travelled. Dad did not want anyone in the house except me and Gene, the church friend. Dad gave Gene my contact information in case something happened at the house while they were away. One night, I got ready for bed and then a text from Gene appeared on my phone. It was a joint text to me and dad that three cars were in the driveway and people were in my parents' house. It was my sister, her husband Kyle, and several more people they allowed in the house. Gene encountered Kyle at the house. Kyle told Gene he was the son-in-law, inferring permission to be there under the family umbrella. Gene relayed that uncomfortable words ensued and held the line with Kyle that no one had permission to be in the house, they needed to leave.

Dad texted me with questions of how Kaylen got into the house, why she was there, when she planned to leave, and if the house was clean. I called and texted Kaylen. There was no answer. Kaylen called me later and told a similar story that she and Kyle had encountered Gene at mom and dad's house. My sister's communication with me was chummy and indirect. She said that she would leave our parents' house soon and hire a house cleaner. She did not say a word about her current living situation.

Initially I thought nothing of Kaylen and Kyle being at my parents' house. Kaylen and Kyle stayed at my parents' house a lot over the years to watch football, have dinner with them, and stay the night or when they travelled to check on the plants.

Dad called me when he was able to get to a phone that could reach the United States. I told him about Kaylen's call, their encounter with Gene, and that they were going to be out of the house soon. Dad unequivocally said that Kaylen and Kyle did not have permission to be in the house. It was the first time I had heard my dad say that Kaylen was not permitted in the house; a clear sign that their relationship had shifted, at least from his perspective.

Perhaps my parents had had enough of Kaylen and Kyle's bullshit; their flakiness, their messy sick dog, their desperation, their disrespect, their checked out presence, and assumptions that they could overuse everything. Maybe it was a trust thing on my dad's part, or possibly mom and dad were on the same page with each other on what they would tolerate. I don't know exactly nor do I know what dad told Gene before he left about Kaylen and her present status in life. It was all swirling about and very confusing.

Dad asked me to check in on the house. The next day I went to my parents' house and like a virtual tour, shot a video from my phone to send to him. I entered my parents' house through the garage. Everything was fine there. Dried muddy boot prints were all over the white tiled entry-way. The laundry lids were open with damp, crusted, unfinished and un-started cycles inside the washer and dryer. A sour smell of moldy wet clothes hung in the air. Worn dirty-kneed pants and crumpled well-worn socks were strewn across the hard wood dining floor in the direction of the laundry room.

Like an out of place pink elephant stanchion, a wooden jewelry box stood alone in the middle of the family room. Necklaces, bracelets and earrings scattered about the white carpeted floor and down the sides. I did not recognize this jewel case or its contents. My parents' bed was unmade and had been slept in. Dried brown dog turds were in the corners of the room peeking out from under the cream colored floor length drapes. Financial statements in dad's office were uncharacteristically scattered over the top of his desk. My head ached, stomach churned and twisted as I recorded this video of my parents plundered home, knowing they would watch from afar; and not be able to do anything about it as they started their holiday.

A couple of days later, Kaylen reached out to me. She said she was at an Anchorage hotel. Her voice was muted and desperate. I suppose I was next up at bat since mom was out of the country with dad and unavailable for her to call to make demands on. I went to the hotel where Kaylen was to see her and assess the situation. I brought grocery bags of ready to eat, no cook high protein finger-type foods of shrimp, and cheese along with gas cards. I saw Kyle range about the hotel lobby on a cell phone as if he was busy doing something or speaking with someone important. I made eye contact with Kaylen who was sitting in the hotel lobby.

To distance ourselves from the din of hotel guests coming and going, we relocated to the hotel's business center and sat in uncomfortable plastic chairs near the bank of computers. Kyle redirected his paces to range around us in our location with a cell phone glued to his ear. Unaware of their living status, financial arrangement of who paid for what with their apartment, I asked Kaylen what was going on. Kaylen said that their rent money had been stolen and they had to leave the apartment. My immediate naïve, rule-following response was to tell her to call the police to report the theft. That was a muddled no-go, since they had allowed the person who stole the money into the apartment. I later realized that had their apartment become a trap house or they were making, buying, or selling drugs and owed people in that world money, the option to call the police was not viable.

I asked where their animals were. Kaylen said they were in the car as they could not afford the pet deposit the hotel charged. Every hour or so one of them went out to start the car to keep the animals warm. I asked how they had paid for the hotel. She said that Kyle's sister had lent them the money. We moved the conversation from the lobby to the privacy of their room.

Their room was a mess of overstuffed travel bags, backpacks, and duffels with dirty clothes strewn all over the room. The bathroom was messy with make-up bottles open and spilled on the vanity counter. I put the bags of food on the shin level table in the middle of the sitting room. Kyle thanked me, plopped down on the couch and immediately scarfed the food as if he had not eaten in months. Kaylen said she wasn't hungry. I sat on a blue vinyl couch next to Kaylen and across from Kyle. We discussed their present living situation and financial circumstance, which was they had been kicked out of the apartment and were homeless, and that both were unemployed with no savings. They needed to get jobs, save money for rent deposits and get back on track to financial stability to apply for another apartment that accepted pets.

I spoke with the hotel front desk clerk and put another week on my credit card. Without thanking me for the food or additional week's stay I had just paid for, Kaylen asked if I had any cash and that she would pay me back. This was the first time Kaylen asked me for money with a false promise to pay me back. It was obvious that she could not pay me back. I gave her what cash I had and felt reassured in my decision to pay for nutritious food and a safe place for her to lay her head.

By mid-week my parents returned. My husband and I picked my parents up from the airport. My parents were a mix of anxiety and defeat, but with somewhat rejuvenated energy from their trip while their minds had been preoccupied with reports of their younger daughter and son-in-law's antics and their ransacked house. While my husband carried my parents' bags, I gave dad the low-down of Kaylen and Kyle's circumstances, their occupancy at the hotel, their story that someone had stolen their rent money and that I had put a couple of nights of a hotel stay on my credit card for them. Dad was all business, and his presence portrayed that he realized that mom needed his protection.

Dad called me the next day and directed me to arrange a meeting with his two daughters. I suggested that we meet at the restaurant next to the hotel they were staying in so that Kaylen would have no excuse not to appear.

We met later that week. Dad had his signature chicken scratch notes on yellow legal pad paper that only I can read of discussion topics and bullet points of how he was willing to proceed in light of the current financial and homeless crisis situation that Kaylen and Kyle had gotten themselves into. While dad and I waited for Kaylen to arrive at the restaurant, he briefed me on the topics that involved me. Dad limited his discussion to Kaylen and spoke of Kyle only in terms of his marriage to Kaylen.

I texted Kaylen that we had a corner booth in the far back corner of the restaurant. Dad and I placed our food orders and I ordered food for Kaylen that I thought she would like. Dad informed me that he would start a bank account that I was to manage for Kaylen's housing. He admonished me never to give her cash. We agreed he would take the lead in this meeting with Kaylen.

Kaylen was her usual late self and strode into the restaurant towards our table with defenses up. With fake confidence she dragged a chair from another table and plopped herself at the edge of table. I welcomed her and said that I had ordered her some food. She snipped that she wasn't hungry. I retorted that she could take it to go back to the room for later. Our quick verbal welcome felt like a hostile micro-aggression, one up, last word exchange.

Kaylen slouched at the table like a troubled defiant teen at a family meeting that couldn't be bothered to talk about why she was late for curfew. Dad asked Kaylen about the stolen rent money. They exchanged names of people they both knew that I didn't. Dad asked about missing oil paintings and art from his house. Kaylen said that she'd ask others that were at the house about the art. Dad confirmed the house was in shambles. Kaylen said she tried to leave it clean but was getting out of there as fast as she could because that was what he had wanted. Dad asked Kaylen to return his house key. Kaylen chucked the house key attached to a paperclip towards dad on the table. Dad checked that item of discussion off his list.

During this exchange, Kaylen's eyes closed and her head bobbed as she nodded and dozed off. I had seen this behavior before with opiate-addicted clients. I brought the nodding off behavior to her attention and she said that she was tired because she hadn't slept. Dad continued down the list and pulled out of his pocket a see-through plastic bag and placed it on the table. It was a bag of needles he had found in his bed. Kaylen started to cry. Dad said he knew that she was in a spot and had a problem. He offered to help with housing until they got their financial feet on the ground; provided they actively sought employment and all discussion about money went through me.

The underpinnings of dads words was a stop gap plan intended to set a framework that would support them and protect mom. With me as the broker of information and financial support gate-keeper between Kaylen and our parents, the money would not be going to drugs. Dad deposited a set amount into an account that I managed for Kaylen's housing until they could get jobs to earn money to support themselves. Kaylen would no longer have access to mom to rage or manipulate for money. From that point forward, my dad always answered the house phone. My mom stopped using a cell phone.

Dad told Kaylen to keep in touch with me as I was the only person that was looking out for her right now. The conversation at the restaurant came to an end with confirmation of her last day at the hotel and dates to relocate to a longer term temporary housing situation.

That next week I searched for affordable week- and month-long housing options. I located a place in downtown Anchorage that was two blocks from my office. I called the manager, who showed me the rooms and hotel facilities. This pay by the week Anchorage hotel seemed perfect. The rooms had a kitchenette, private shower, and bathroom with nice views. The laundry, exercise facilities, and parking were safe and near local businesses, restaurants, coffee shops, and schools for Kaylen and Kyle to work, earn money, and get back on their feet. I gave the manager my card, contact information, and advance paid for four weeks.

I returned to my office and texted Kaylen that I had put dad's budgeted money down on affordable temporary housing for a couple of weeks and suggested a meet up to explain the terms of the new housing. I reveled in my win for the day and shifted into day job work mode and checked my email. The hotel Kaylen and Kyle checked out of sent an email that my card was charged additional fees because pets were in the room. So much for paying me back. Addiction 2, Kelleybury's 0.

6

Hapless Hunt For Housing

ONE WEEKDAY AFTER WORK, I met Kaylen and Kyle at a coffee shop in a super-market to sit down and discuss with them the temporary housing I secured for them, dads deal, and to obtain an update on efforts they had made towards getting jobs. I entered the store through the sliding glass doors and saw Kaylen standing at the coffee area with a shopping cart. Kyle ranged about the deli, pretending to be interested in the specialty cheeses and olives while eyeing the comings and goings of customers. He nodded at me as confirmation that he saw me. There were no tables and chairs to sit and discuss the matters before us. I went to Kaylen and asked, "Where'd all the tables and chairs go?"

Her heavy lidded eyes barely made contact with mine. The tint of the store lights exposed caked-on makeup that covered peeled skin and blemishes that spotted her face. Her long brown, mousy dry hair was styled with a side part to obscure her irritated red receding hairline. A delicate black lace choker crossed her neck. Through her stained yellow teeth and bright pink-lip sticked mouth, she perceptively said, "They don't want people hanging around. They want people to get their shit and get the fuck out of their store." This knowing insight came from her like the new pair of street smart shoes she wore.

I could tell that Kaylen and Kyle had been at the store for a while, as the cart was filled with non-essential crap; a diffuser, a mug, and beauty products. Well, nonessential for me. I suppose for those with severe substance use disorders, that stuff may seem essential. Like twin teenaged siblings, Kaylen and Kyle chided each other on what was a necessary item and what was not. I wondered how they were going to pay for the items, being they were unemployed and homeless.

"Why buy a mug when I just gave you one for your birthday?" I asked as a roundabout dignified prompt in effort to avoid addressing the current destitute situation they were in. That was my older sister way of indirectly asking how they were going to pay for all of the items without directly asking her that question.

"What mug?" she asked, as her eyes swayed away from me.

"The white mug with gold fringe with the cute little pink bird on it, remember?"

"It broke," she vacantly replied, again without eye contact.

I didn't believe her. My heart sank. Not only was she lying to me, I specially selected that birthday gift for her with the thought that it was hopeful and would brighten her mornings as I was trying so desperately to do right then. The birthday gift I gave her meant more to me than it did her. It all meant more to me than it did her, everything; her housing, her health, her marriage, her employment status and lack thereof, her life. At least I could hold onto the sibling bond notion that she wouldn't look me in the eye and lie. I rationalized in the trinity of my heart, mind, and soul that the white lies that passed by the black choker she wore across her neck were harmless finesses that saved face from the truth of the homeless, drug addicted path she treaded.

Kaylen was all business; unconcerned with the housing details. I supplied her with the hotel address along with the manager's name and gave her the parking permit, keys, and house rules. There was no discussion of their efforts to obtain employment.

The next morning the hotel manager called. She said she didn't think it was going to work out with my sister and brother-in-law.

"What do you mean?" I asked.

"Their car is parked in the wrong place. Your sister's husband is acting weird, and there are a lot of people coming and going out of their room," she said.

I told the hotel manager that I gave all the information of parking details and such to Kaylen, not Kyle, and that may be why the car was in the wrong space. I explained to her that I had spoken with my sister and her husband probably didn't hear what was said about house rules, quiet hours, and parking. I asked the hotel manager to allow me the opportunity to stop by the hotel later that afternoon to confirm that they understood the house rules and parking. Reluctantly, she agreed.

After work I met with Kaylen and Kyle in the hotel lobby. Kaylen's arms were defensively crossed in front of her as her mouth pursed and eyes rolled at Kyle's restless behavior. I explained that I had received a call from the hotel manager. Without allowing me to finish my sentence, Kaylen interrupted and said, "She's a bitch. They're always up our ass and in our business for something, judging and no privacy."

"Kaylen, she's been helpful under the circumstances. I gave you the house rules and the parking permit. Did you show those to Kyle?" I asked.

"I don't know where they are," Kaylen snapped.

It dawned on me and Kyle that he did not know that he had violated the hotel's parking and quiet hour rules. I leaned towards Kyle and in a low voice said, "There are cameras all around. They are watching you all the time." Like a precocious seven-year-old, Kaylen nonsensically spouted off something about privacy, judgments, and grown ass adults that can have guests and visitors anytime they wanted.

"I'm not going to engage in this right now, Kaylen. I suggest the two of you find alternative affordable housing and jobs as soon as possible. You are on borrowed time," I said without equivocation.

The following Monday, the hotel manager called and said, "This is not going to work. I see on the video your brother-in-law is coming and going at all hours of the night and hovers around their car with people that are not hotel guests."

I explained that my sister and brother-in-law had pets in the car and probably went to the car to check on them. The hotel manager blurted, "He's acting like a drug dealer. I can't have that on my property. I'm sorry; this is not going to work. I'll refund you the difference. I'm sorry it went this way. Good luck to your sister. I hope she will be safe. She mentioned they'd have to go back to living in the car."

"Oh, okay. I appreciate your candor," I said. "I'll be by this week to refund the difference on my card."

I ended the call with a feeling of suspended animation. It was a gut punch to hear from an outside person that did not have history with Kyle that he was a drug dealer. I didn't want to believe that Kyle sold drugs. I liked Kyle. I cared about Kyle. I saw his inability to control his drinking. The first time he came to Alaska to meet our family, he drank too much, left the restaurant and got lost on the streets of Anchorage in wintertime. My husband and brother-in-law had to go find him.

I knew alcoholism ran in his family. Kaylen and Kyle's graduation was the first time I had met Kyle's younger brother; he was a bumbling laughing drunk, spitting his food when he talked about how nice it was to finally meet the older sister Kaylen had talked about. Kyle's parents were separated at the time and in the process of an awkward, bitter divorce. I chalked the brother's drunkenness up to how that family coped during difficult times.

At Kaylen and Kyle's wedding, Kyle's dad drunkenly chased my auntie around the reception hall. When Kyle worked at my office, people asked if he was using drugs due to his nervous energy and profuse sweating. I rationalized that in all the years I had known Kyle, he always had a lot of physical energy and sweated a lot. Kyle had been a college athlete with high energy. I was not a sports girl, so I chalked that up to his natural disposition. Eventually, I had to let Kyle go from work at my office because he was always late, projects were unfinished or done half-assed with explanations that his way was better. My dad's friends also had to fire him. They said he was selling drugs in the parking lot. My sister's life-long friends said Kyle supplied drugs. So, looking back on it all now, the hotel manager's words and observations were independent corroboration of what I could not see through the rose colored lenses I wore. There were so many clues that Kyle had problems with substance abuse. I didn't recognize the behavior for what it was.

Later that day my sister texted that Kyle had found an apartment and the landlord wanted to speak with me about the rental deposit. For his part, Kyle landed an apartment in the same complex as his younger brother. Kyle forwarded me the contact information to speak with the landlord, confirm the apartment location and rent amount, and transfer that amount from the account I had set up with funds dad supplied to the landlord's LLC account. I clarified that I was not signing the lease. The rent was subsidized from a conservator-type account. Over the next couple of days Kaylen and Kyle moved into the apartment he found. I was hopeful that from a place of stable housing, Kaylen and Kyle would have space to secure jobs and get back on their feet.

Kaylen's lifelong friend Julee and I coordinated appearances at the apartment. We showed up with groceries, dog food, and walked Kaylen's hundred pound husky malamute mix dog with her in sly effort to assess Kaylen's level of instability. Everything in Kaylen's life was unstable, especially her mood. She was angry, bossy, and mean. She was still unemployed, every other week she was in jail, her marriage was co-dependent, and her environment had become publicly hostile and ugly.

Kaylen and Kyle's relationship grew increasingly toxic, with in your face social media posts of infidelity and physical abuse. The frenzy, fury, betrayals, and domestic violence reached a fever pitch and Kyle moved to the upstairs apartment with his brother while Kaylen remained in the downstairs apartment with her dog. On several occasions Kyle and his younger brother called the police to report Kaylen, citing domestic abuse. Kaylen was arrested and jailed. Kaylen's friends forwarded the latest police blotters of Kaylen to me. Initially I cringed at every ding on my phone. I then prompted myself to drink a glass of water at each ding, and to go to the garden to get grounded, as self care measures that would not distract me to Kaylen's crises.

When Kaylen was in jail I looked up her court date and the charges. I called dad to inform him of the latest police and court system encounters and regroup. It's odd to feel relief when your loved one is in jail rather than kicking around town crazy and viciously high.

I reached out to my public defender friends to determine how the criminal charges might unfold and whether Kaylen's case could be directed to "therapeutic drug court" for forced rehab. I was embarrassed to call my lawyer friends about criminal charges against my sister. I attended law school with many of them and they had known our family for decades. We've supported and mentored each other in our respective practice areas and worked cases together over the years. I awkwardly clarified to the receptionist that my call was a personal matter. Each graciously took my call.

It was a challenge to overcome my emotions and swallow my shame to discuss the nuts and bolts of the legal predicaments Kaylen faced. My colleagues informed me which law group was assigned to Kaylen's criminal case and explained that the charges against her did not directly involve drugs, so the drug court rehab program was not an option. As the informative conversation wound to an end, my public defender lawyer friends gingerly suggested that I dampen my hopeful commitment to my sister's plight. Having had experience with substance dependency in their lives, and worked with drug abuse in their profession, they shared stories from a realist perspective and introduced me to the concept of "**loving from afar.**" I am so appreciative of their kind, nonjudgmental words, assistance, and support from their heart to mine so that my heart would not be continually broken. Ultimately charges against Kaylen were dismissed, as a case cannot be prosecuted without a complaining witness who was her drug addicted husband.

Within two months, the landlord of the apartment Kyle found left the following message:

"Sorry Michaela to bother you, this is Kaylen's landlord. We spoke once before. You need to call me about her. This is a big mess. I should have known better. Please give me a call back." Addiction 3, Kelley-burys 0.

7

Incite Intervention

WITH EACH PASSING DAY, Kaylen's drug dependency continued to devolve with crisis upon crisis as her life spiraled into a nose dive. Her social media posts included raw details of her relationship with Kyle, fraught with viciousness, betrayals, and infidelities. Her environment was increasingly unstable and her behavior was erratic. She remained unemployed, was in the process of being evicted from the apartment Kyle found, and had spent her retirement savings on drugs.

Julee and I felt that the level of instability in Kaylen's life presented a window of opportunity for an effective intervention; especially with Kyle's separation from Kaylen to his brother's upstairs apartment. I shared this information with my parents. They had finally opened up to each other and to the possibility that there was a chance to save Kaylen, or at least a way that would not give up on or abandon her. As they gained understanding about substance dependency and how it evolved into abuse and misuse with Kaylen, they re-entered the community. Their energy and relationship shifted. They had some hope.

Mom, dad, Julee and I arranged to meet at a Chinese restaurant after work to regroup about Kaylen. It was the same restaurant mom had taken me and Kaylen to when I was in high school thirty years earlier. I arrived late to the restaurant and heard Julee's high-pitched giggle from across the room. I bustled past the aquarium toward the table in the back corner of the dimly lit dining area, and shimmied into the red vinyl seat next to Julee.

Julee was happy to see mom and dad, and they were happy to see her too. It had been over a year since they had seen each other. Julee, her husband and daughter always came to my parents' house to celebrate Kaylen's birthday, but hadn't attended last December because Kaylen's condition was too far gone.

Julee was a sphere of bright light for my parents, outfitted in a stylish yet professional pink shirt and black slacks. Her naturally curly, long blonde hair was pulled back with a clip that exposed her sparkling blue eyes behind the trendy glasses she wore. She had a big smile on her face after having updated my parents on the precocious antics of her beloved pre-school-aged daughter.

I settled into the booth, and before I could catch a breath or look at the menu, dad fired questions at me in cop-like fashion over the cheetah print reading glasses he took from mom that hung crooked on his face. He wanted to know whether Kaylen had a job and whether she signed conservator and divorce papers. My jaw defensively clinched and my shoulders tensed up to my ears. I sank into the oversized seat cushion feeling like a failure for not meeting my father's expectations.

Julee spit out water on the glass covered table, shriek laughed out loud and said, "Well, *that* will never happen!"

Mom and dad stared blankly across the table at me and Julee, stunned at the thought that Kaylen in this world of addiction would not adhere to the dictates they felt should fall into place the way they thought was best. Julee's light and genuine comeback was exactly what was needed to jolt me out of my conscientious people-pleasing manner and my dad out of his large and in charge missives.

"Well then what are we here for?" dad asked.

"We're here to discuss an intervention with Kaylen, dad. Every time you tell me to get her to sign divorce and conservator papers and it's not done, I feel like a failure," I told him. "I can't make Kaylen sign divorce and conservator papers any more than I can make you sign your antique car or truck over to me."

And with that, dad sat back and opened his mind to rehabilitation for his younger daughter and considered a plan that included his participation in an intervention. My parents' started to realize that we're all adults, including Kaylen, who would do and not do whatever she or we wanted. There was nothing my parents' could do except their part. It was a breath of fresh air with Julee by my side that inspired me to switch the approach of how to interact with my parents and Kaylen.

The conversation moved to the nuts and bolts of an intervention, with the end goal being getting Kaylen into treatment. There are several moving parts to an intervention that include who will participate, when the intervention will occur, location of the intervention, how to facilitate an addict's admittance to a program, and what happens at discharge or graduation from a program, each of which requires consideration.

Mom and dad agreed to pay for John's services as a professional interventionist. They also agreed to research local rehab treatment options, as Kaylen was an unemployed adult with no insurance. The four of us discussed who would be on the intervention team and contingencies for potential hurdles that Kaylen might assert to entering rehab, including foster care of Kaylen's dog and two cats.

I committed to reach out to John to coordinate a time frame for an intervention. Julee maintained contact with Kaylen and her other soul sister girlfriends to keep a finger on the pulse of Kaylen's stability and to funnel more support towards an intervention and getting her into treatment. Later that night when I arrived home, I told my husband Chris about the plan and we discussed the level of our children's participation. Chris agreed to speak with our children about the level of participation they could contribute while they were away at school.

John arrived in Alaska and planned to stay for a week to prepare, educate, and coordinate our team on the nitty-gritty of what an intervention entails. An intervention team has to be creative and collaborative on how to engage and be with each other, and ultimately the addict, in a group setting. Considerations of locations for an intervention and facilities for treatment and rehab facilities, associated costs, payment, insurance, transportation, and other types of support of a loved one that agrees to go to rehab were some of the things we discussed.

John's first assignment was for us to watch the video again. Next was to write letters to Kaylen, and we were to bring those to the next meeting we had with John. The letters would be read to Kaylen at the intervention describing how addiction had destroyed the person we love and the relationship each of us had with her. The letter was not an opportunity to criticize, dump anger or guilt her with a list of humiliations and disappointments. The gist was to let her know that we knew she had a problem, but that we care for and love her and are willing to help. The intervention letter had to include non-negotiable boundaries in the event the help we were prepared to offer Kaylen was not accepted. We each went home to dutifully embark on writing our letters.

I struggled to concentrate on writing a love letter to Kaylen about her addicted drug life of chaos. My mind jumped to the business I had to run and client case matters that I was responsible for. I felt that there was not enough time to devote to this venture, and that Kaylen had already absorbed so much of my time and energy. Those were convenient lies and excuses I told myself to keep all the feelings I had about addiction and how it got a hold on my sister bottled up. It took great effort to step back into a place of love for Kaylen; to let feelings flow from my heart to the pen and onto paper. My "type A" legal writing and helicopter mom mind wrestled with uncontrollable spheres of doubt, fear, and uncertainty. Initially, I took the safe route and wrote a script in attempt to talk over my fear of rejection.

I hoped that an intervention would work, but I also felt a heavy cloud of doubt that maybe Kaylen was too far down the rabbit hole of addiction. My heart sank to my toes and deeper to the center of the earth with the thought that Kaylen would choose drugs and an addicted life-style over our family, our relationship, and life itself. It's a hard task to write a letter to someone you love while simultaneously steeling yourself for rejection. It was challenging to set boundaries with my sister, since I was the one that had taken care of her most of my life and all of hers. Right sizing the larger than life feelings of responsibility and obligation to support, protect, and save my sister was a difficult process and one I continue to struggle with every day. Another hurdle was my inability to envision how the intervention would end. I had no control over the outcome and it was scary.

I practiced MWBT and introduced the RFF of fear to my mustard seed grain of faith. I prayed that the combined loving spirit of our family and friends for Kaylen would plant seeds of recovery within her. The introduction of fear to faith created a chemistry of courage to step into my best vulnerable self with abiding love and a super-power ability to unearth the deep seeded and entangled roots of what had become our distant relationship. I wept writing the letter and set pragmatic boundaries that fit for me. I arrived at the conclusion that all I could do was control myself; how I stepped into the room, how I showed up, what I would say, and how I would be in relationship with her in the state she was in.

Eight of us dutifully wrote letters that recalled loving moments with Kaylen and drew continued relationship lines in the sand. Kaylen's lifelong friends wrote letters of their support and hopeful prayers that she would agree to treatment. John said my fourteen-year-old daughter's letter was the best. My heart inflated with the infusion of love and support from my husband, our children, my parents, and my sister's lifelong friends. The words each placed onto the pages expressed their individual slice of love with thoughtfully selected boundaries and the caveat that we would no longer be riding on the crazy train of crisis and chaos that she was conducting. We were getting off at the next stop and hoped she would come with us.

Dad explained to John that his research of treatment and local rehab programs had waiting lists several months long, and that there was a qualifying process for the severity/level of substance abuse. John discussed the costs and locations of rehab facilities outside of the state of Alaska, worked with my parents to locate a rehab treatment facility that had space for Kaylen, and identified facilities that could take her on as a patient. Next, John explained the process of an intervention.

At the next meeting with John we strategized. Mom and Julee felt Kaylen would bolt from the intervention, or agree to go to rehab and leave once they arrived to be with Kyle's family in the lower forty-eight as some sort of weird leverage over Kyle. The fear of losing Kaylen was real. Each of us were scared she would reject our pleas to get her help. We all felt like Noah building the arc after being warned catastrophic events to come, not knowing where we were going but moving forward anyways with blind faith and pure hope.

The six of us brainstormed potential encounters with Kaylen and discussed how to arrange our appearances at the same place. We knew that she was motivated by money and that the landlord was in the process of kicking her out of the apartment. We focused on an encounter around paying for temporary housing and planned to appear at the apartment complex she was getting kicked out of under the auspices of helping her move.

Earlier that day I had received a call from an unknown number. It was Kaylen. She said she had a flat tire and asked me to electronically transfer $150 to her account so that she could fix the tire. I knew this was a ploy to extract cash from me so I deflected and told her that I didn't do the electronic banking thing. But it gave us the excuse to show up at the apartment under the guise of helping her fix her vehicle and move out. We would tell her that we had temporary housing for her, and hopefully get her on a plane to rehab. My husband would be with me under the auspices of taking a look at what was wrong with my sister's car. My parents planned to show up in dad's truck under the pretense of helping to move boxes and furniture.

We next discussed how to get Kaylen to a rehab facility out of state. Julee volunteered to fly with my sister to personally deliver her to rehab. The rationale was that we believed that Kaylen would go on a trip with her girlfriend, but not me or my parents. Mom volunteered her airline miles to the cause. The next hurdle was that Kaylen perpetually lost her identification and would not be able to board a plane. We figured how to get a temporary form of identification with the birth certificate and other identifiers my parents had on file for Kaylen to get her on a plane. Chris coordinated flights using mom's airline miles to the place John had found that had an available bed. Chris waited on the phone for hours and spoke with a complete stranger in another state that could hear the desperation in his voice.

We reserved two conjoined hotel rooms; one for Kaylen to occupy and the other for John to conduct the intervention. I brought a travel bag for Kaylen to use that I filled with toiletries, self-care items, and clothes to wear while she was in rehab. Doubtful that she would accept our offer, I left the tags on the items to make returns in the event she rejected our offer to help.

As we excitedly put the finishing touches on the plan, mom non-chalantly revealed that she had given Kaylen $300 earlier that day. The energy in the room immediately plummeted. Each of us stood gob-smacked by mom's disclosure. Our hope dashed with the realization that there was no incentive for Kaylen to participate in an intervention if she had money for her next fix. Mom's action of giving Kaylen cash neutralized the only incentive we could think of to draw Kaylen to a meeting with us.

My dad was pissed and defeated, while my mom shrank in her seat, repeatedly mumbling "I'm sorry. I did something wrong. I was bad."

It became oddly apparent that mom suffered from something greater than emotional overwhelm and trauma of Kaylen's addiction. Mom's confession exposed a vulnerable link, and in that moment we each realized that link was being exploited and that we had to protect mom. We regrouped and navigated a work around for this new development.

Mom was the prototypical enabler and vulnerable to Kaylen's asks. To say financial support of my sister was a tiff between my parents would be an understatement. Mom always gave Kaylen money. My sister had never been financially independent. It got to the point where Kaylen raged at and guilted our mom into giving her money for "medication." My sister's sick, self-medicating mind convinced herself that she could manage between meth and heroin. Mom, not knowing any better, believed my sister's sick words and wanted her pain and anxiety relieved, and so gave her hundreds of dollars.

We planned the intervention for a Thursday to get my sister on a plane for a three-and-a-half-hour flight to Seattle and to check into a rehab facility with sufficient time to manage withdrawals and detox over the weekend when most places are closed. As the day came to a close, we reviewed the schedule for the next day and decided to meet at the hotel and drive caravan style to the apartment complex. My husband and I closed the office and in the exhausted state we were in, picked up take out for dinner to eat at home.

It was late by the time we arrived home. Chris and I ate our fried chicken dinner and silently contemplated the next day's events. There was one last decision for the day; what to wear to an intervention.

Clothes selection is an important decision. The next morning goes more smoothly when clothes are pre-selected. Like scaffolding to a building, clothes can structure and inform the day. Despite my emotionally fatigued mind and physically exhausted body, I knew clothing for intervention day called for something strong, powerful, comfortable, and accessible in the event there was an encounter with Kyle or other junkies.

When I select outfits, I focus on the event, consider the weather and build from there. I wasn't feeling that there was a right or wrong color for an intervention and it wasn't a holiday or formal speaking event. I started with footwear and decided it was the perfect opportunity to wear the cowboy boots I bought when I was in Wyoming. I considered the boots my "shit-kickers" so I could kick the shit out of addiction, and built my outfit around the cowboy boots with a pair of boot cut jeans, a brown Boho shirt with a walrus ivory necklace, and porcelain flower earrings that were my Aunt Chrissie's, dads sister and my sister's god-mother that somehow throughout the years landed in my jewelry box. I set my clothes by the shower.

I returned to the bedroom and sat at the edge of my bed to mentally review the Jenga pieces of the next day that our intervention team had carefully planned. I felt a heavy cross to bear due to the density of my obligation. I didn't want any of this responsibility, but there I was feeling shouldered with it. I just wanted my sister and our family back. I was afraid Kaylen would refuse our help. I was afraid Kaylen would reject us. I prayed everything would fall into place and come together, and that we would find her and connect. I checked my phone before saying prayers to Sts. Michael and Maximillian to cast out the darkness of doubt in my heart and replace it with an armor of light as I lay down to rest. My eyes welled and heart warmed as I scrolled through text upon text from family and friends that extended strength and well wishes for the next day. Team Kelleybury rallied and got stronger.

8

The Day Before Us

I'M WHAT THE SLEEP SCIENCE FOLKS CALL A LARK. Mornings are my jam. Mornings are a special time of day that starts early for me. I'm the first one up before anyone else in the house, except for maybe the fish. Living in wooded mountains makes each morning feel like I'm the first human up in the whole wide world. Mornings are quiet, usually dark and there are no demands; just a fresh clean day for me to step into. I feel that all other times of the day are for everyone else and mornings were made especially for me.

Mornings are sacred. I have a sanctified morning routine that sets a footing to preserve this precious time of day so that I may walk through the other hours of the day with a signature swing for whatever enters my sphere of influence. Each morning starts with warm lemon water to swig down vitamins in an intentionally selected glass. Then I wander through the house to fill diffusers with water placed in key areas throughout my home and deliberately select the oil that will enhance my day. Yes, my day; my way. I stop by the sink to wash my face, and then park myself on the big brown cloth puffy recliner chair to meditate, contemplate, and journal. I return to the kitchen to prepare a perfect cup of coffee and, if I feel it, flow into a mini stretch routine while the coffee processes. Depending on the day, meaning whether it snows and taking into account the status of the other house occupants' health, wellness, and daily itinerary, this morning ritual can span twenty to thirty, sometimes forty or sixty minutes. On blessed days that routine can expand to one hundred twenty minutes.

Today was intervention day and this morning was elevated to a distinct class. From the moment my eyes opened, I felt I was in a marshmallow; a sticky, pully drag on moving in any direction, especially forward, whatever moving forward meant on this day. I warmed the water and reflected on how much each member of the intervention team contributed to the undertaking which was now before us. My heart was full of gratitude for each individual commitment to Kaylen's wellbeing. I swallowed what felt like horse pills of daily vitamins, squeezed the lemon into a mug of water and rubbed some of the sweet citrus juice on my hands and face to absorb even a small bit of nontoxic purity to begin this pensive day. I shuffled from the kitchen to the puffy brown chair. I lit a candle, selected the diffuser oil, and thought to myself, this is definitely a Frankincense day. My merry Mary Yogini always says, "When in doubt, Frankincense."

That morning I was laden with doubt. I sat in the quiet, dense morning space while uncontrollable factors surfaced and deluged me like a waterfall of never-ending "what ifs" that pummeled my brain from a 60-foot drop of uncertainty of what the day would bring.

My 95-pound dog Clyde rested his head on my lap and stared into my eyes like only Clyde does, knowing what this human in his life needed in the moment. Paw by paw Clyde climbed onto me and the chair, with an oversized attempt to wedge himself onto my disproportionately smaller sized lap all while I steadfastly endeavored to meditate. Clyde's unabashed intrusiveness in my sacred morning space filled the empty, insecure, and alone feelings of my soul. Clyde gave up trying to fit into the recliner with me and changed course to the bedroom to cuddle with my husband. I resumed a loving kindness meditation with prayers to Sts. Jude and Maximillian, the patron saints of lost causes and addiction I had prayed to for my sister in the previous weeks. I heard rustling, snorting, jingling and murmuring to the left and felt the air and energy of the room fluctuate. I opened my eyes and there, like three stanchions, stood my husband and our two dogs Bonnie and Clyde with a knowing silent presence.

My husband went to the kitchen and did his own morning routine of feeding the dogs, while making himself a cup of coffee and the signature tea he makes for me. Quietly within the confines of our own minds, my husband and I showered, dressed, and readied for the day. We printed our letters and mutely rehearsed delivery of the words we wrote on the pages as we paced around the bed and bathroom. With tear-filled eyes, Chris read the letter our teenagers had written in front of a full length mirror. I continued to ready myself for the day at the sink. He turned to me and asked, "Is it okay to cry? I don't think I can help myself."

I looked at him and thought, *there is no way I could love this man any more than I do right now.* "I think it is," I gently responded, "all we can do is be who we are."

The forty-minute drive to town was dense and silent; no radio, only road noise. Chris parked the car in the frost-covered parking lot of the hotel where we had reserved rooms for John and the intervention. Upon arrival, my phone lit up with texts and calls from dad and Julee that Kaylen was at the apartment she was getting kicked out of and that we needed to get over there right then. In that change of plans moment, the pre-planned intervention location of a mid-town hotel suite switched to my sister's apartment on the other side of town. John hopped in the backseat of our car for the drive across town. Anxiety rushed and stirred within me. *I know this feeling,* I thought to myself, *it's a red flag feeling; a sign to slow down, pause and collect the loving purposeful energy within my heart and soul and to connect with what is higher in this moment rather than be carried away in the rush of the moment.*

Within the angst-filled tense confines of the car, I asked, "Are you guys okay with me praying before we head over there?"

The air and space within the car neutralized, and without hesitation John said, "Yes, please do!"

And so there in the hotel parking lot, the three of us leaned into the car's center console and connected in each other's presence for what we were about to embark upon. I coined a mantra in that moment to prepare for the worst while hoping and praying for the best; as reality usually falls somewhere in between.

Normally I'm not the kumbaya-type of person that prays with other people; especially a man I recently met in person and don't know that well. As spirituality goes, I'm quiet and to myself with prayers and intentions. In fact, the only other time I prayed with my husband was fifteen years prior to this moment, and that was for our then three-year-old son who was to have surgery. In that moment I prayed for strength and grace to carry us through the day. "Please help us find her and grace us with the spirit to motivate her to treatment. Instill hope and faith of recovery," I implored.

On the drive to the apartment, we each considered what we would do when we saw Kaylen. I suggested that I take the lead and tell Kaylen that we were there to help move her out of the apartment and fix the flat tire on her car that she had called me about. Chris parked the car at the ice covered visitors parking area to the side of the apartment complex and expressed concern about the neighborhood and security of the car. He grabbed the tire iron as a legit prop for our encounter, but also for personal safety. I saw dad's red truck parked at the corner of the street and spotted Julee. She and I walked towards each other and naturally stepped to the front to lead the pack while Chris, dad, mom and John fell in line behind us. Julee and I nervously murmured to each other:

Me: "What are we going to do/say?"

Julee: "I don't know, I've never done an intervention before."

Me: "Neither have I. We'll just tell her that we're here to help her move, which is a true and genuine statement. That's not a lie. You know me; I'm not a good liar so I just don't do it."

Just then Kaylen darted in front of us between the apartment complex and her car in the tenant parking area.

Julee yelled, "Hey girl, we're here to help you move."

Me: "Yeah, and I brought Chris so he could take a look at your car and fix the tire you said was broken."

Kaylen: "Oh hey, I don't need your help anymore. I can take care of it myself. What are mom and dad doing here? Who's that guy?" she asked looking at John.

Me: "I brought mom and dad with dad's truck to help you move."

John stepped through the pack and said, "Kaylen, I'm John, an interventionist, and I'm here to help."

"Oh no, I'm not doing this right now," Kaylen said, and she bolted into the apartment building.

The six of us followed her into the dingy basement apartment. The door and frame to the unit were busted; validation that her social media posts of the physical violence and continued demise of her marriage to Kyle had devolved into base, destructive relations. The apartment was cold, dank, mostly empty, and reeked of urine with dirty walls and stains all over the light-colored shag carpet.

The group of us stood in the apartment entryway like a human wall that blocked Kaylen's exit. Without making eye contact with any of us, Kaylen scurried around the apartment to the few remaining objects in there, such as her purse, phone, a pile of clothes and her oversized malamute dog.

Kaylen paced about the apartment and said, "I'm not doing this right now. I don't have time. I have to get out of here. I have things to do."

John stepped forward and said, "Kaylen, your family is here to talk to you; they are concerned about you and want to help you."

"I know exactly who and what you are and what you all want to do. You must know the statistics that interventions rarely work. In fact 90% of them fail. I don't have time for this and I'm not doing this right now. I have to move out this apartment right now so please move out of my way," Kaylen sputtered at John.

"We're not moving, Kaylen," dad steadfastly announced.

None of the six of us moved. With feigned attention on gathering what little belongings remained in the apartment, Kaylen frenetically bustled around the living room area. The six of us stood solid and watched her fruitless efforts to make the next move. Her dog broke the tension when he peed on the carpeted floor. Just then, Kaylen bolted to the window, opened it, climbed out and ran away from the apartment. Her phone fell out of her back pocket. Chris turned and ran up the stairs and out of the complex to follow Kaylen.

Julee, my parents and I stepped into the apartment. I picked up Kaylen's phone and purse. Mom muttered discouraging I-told-you-so type words to dad. Julee and I rationalized out loud that Kaylen would not get too far without her phone and that she would never leave her dog, and we had taken the whole day off from work with nowhere else to go and so we decided to just wait her out. I handed Kaylen's purse and phone to Julee and went up the stairs to see whether Chris caught up with Kaylen.

Chris and Kaylen stood in front of each other in the alley behind the apartment building. Chris's arms were extended with his hands on Kaylen's shoulders. Kaylen's head hung low between Chris's arms with her arms by her side. He spoke to her and she listened. Later, Chris shared with me what he said to Kaylen in that pivotal alley moment:

"Kaylen, I love you. We all love you and that is why we are here. It scares the hell out me what is happening to you. I'm worried about you and your safety. I'm afraid you're living out *Requiem for a Dream* and you're going to end up like that."

"I'm not living out *Requiem for a Dream*," Kaylen said to Chris.

"Kaylen, the people that love you most are here for you and have good, positive things to say to you. At a minimum you owe it to your family to at least listen to what we have to say. It won't kill you to listen to what we have to say. Humor me and listen to what we have to say. You can take it or leave it. It's not a waste of time and it is good to hear from people that love you most," Chris requested of Kaylen.

With his right arm around Kaylen's shoulder, they returned to the apartment. Chris told the group, "Kaylen has agreed to listen to us. I told her that we are all here for her, that we love her, and invested a lot to be here today because we love and care about her."

With that, Chris and Kaylen entered the apartment and closed the door.

Kaylen's head was low. She did not make eye contact with any of us. She stepped to the side of Chris, and slid down to a seated position with her back against the wall, while she stared at the floor. When her butt connected with the floor, she raised her head and said, "Okay, go ahead, start."

The six of us fell into horseshoe formation in front of her. A large moat of emotional space was between us. Chris sat in front of the door and my dad was seated in a rickety, undersized collapsible chair next to him. John was at the center, Julee sat on her knees next to John, then mom and I sat with the dog behind us.

Chris went first. He relayed helpless feelings when he heard me cry each morning, the despair within our family, the grief and heavy worry carried over the past several months from her years of addiction. He asked Kaylen to agree to get help and said the reason for the "boundaries" he and I had agreed upon if she would not agree to get help was to protect our children. Chris explained in his written and spoken words to Kaylen that her lifestyle and the people she was around were dangerously unhealthy and that we could not expose our children to that. He told her that he loved her but that she was not welcome at our house while she continued to use drugs, and that we would not allow our children to be in her presence while she used drugs.

Chris next channeled the sweet presence of our children with their innocent heart-felt-words to their auntie of the role she held in their lives and with hopeful pleas requested that she accept the help our family offered to get her into treatment. Our kids promised to support Kaylen if she attended treatment with visits, letters, and care packages. Their sweet salutary words caught in Chris's chest as he tearfully choked out that they would always be her best man and little flower girl. Tears streamed down my sister's face as Chris read the words from our daughter.

Next was dad, who pragmatically stated the obvious of Kaylen's inability to hold down a job, that she had spent all her retirement savings on drugs, damaged her mind and body, and demolished her marriage and her health as well as her emotional and social well-being. Dad offered to pay for rehab, transportation, and housing until she completed rehab and got on her feet again. Dad's boundary was that he would no longer financially support her while she used drugs and was in active addiction.

Mom brought two eight by ten framed photos of Kaylen that she set out in front of her before she read her letter to Kaylen. The photos were of when Kaylen was Ms. Teen Alaska and played college soccer. Mom asked to have her beautiful, healthy, and athletic daughter back.

When it came to my turn, I relayed all the times I was stood up by her over the years, now knowing why, and set the boundary that I would no longer support or help or rescue Kaylen. No longer would I make the calls to get charges against her dismissed or get her out of jail without a record that traced back to her. I read a letter from one of Kaylen's lifelong soul sister friends that included similar stories of being stood up when Kaylen was arrested for drugs and times she went to Kaylen's apartment to check on her because she was worried and found her non-responsive and reeking of cat pee. Julee read her letter and a letter from another lifelong friend about the depth and breadth of their friendships.

I don't remember how the intervention ended. It wasn't dramatic, hostile or mean. I recall that Kaylen tearfully expressed if we cared so much for her, we would help mend her marriage and husband, too. Dad said that we were there for her, not Kyle. We had said our piece. She left the apartment, and John reminded each of us to stick to the boundaries we set. We each left and within an hour Kaylen texted me and dad:

> I appreciate the help and I am not opposed to getting help and staying clean—my recent efforts have been in that direction. It may not happen the way you want it but you know I have to do things my own way.

Dad responded to Kaylen's text to let John know when she wanted help with treatment and rehab.

I was drained after the intervention, but even more certain that all that could be done had been done. Kaylen knew that we knew addiction had its grip on her. I possessed great faith that the intervention made an impact and that we planted seeds within her spirit. Each of the writer's gave permission to include their letters in this book to be of use to others and they are included in the appendix. Addiction 3, Kelleyburys 1.

9

Seeds of Recovery

THE MORNING AFTER THE INTERVENTION I was at an odd place with a curious calm. The view outside my window held low clouds that sat heavy like my heart. A cool spring rain exposed the still-frozen brown ground halfway up the mountain with a clear, stabilizing view of the foothills blanketed with frosty dew over the naked leafless trees. A raw, early spring chill held in the air; it was as if Mother Nature held my spirit in suspended animation. A light snow lay on the top half of the highland mount, its peak cloaked behind clouds; similar to my relationship with my sister, I knew it was there, but the terrain leading to the summit was clouded and unknown. What Mother Nature created and painted on the outside world synchronized with how I felt inside. My hands and feet were cold, and I felt lighter with half the weight of my sister's addicted world lifted from my shoulders; left at base camp for Kaylen to choose her own route.

My parents thought the intervention was unsuccessful since Kaylen did not accept the help we offered. I felt differently. I felt that half the battle was that Kaylen would deny that she had a problem with drugs and addiction. Kaylen is smart, had obtained advanced degrees and worked in drug treatment centers with experience regarding drugs, addiction, and mental health matters and could word smith anyone out of a conversation focused on the complexity of addiction. I felt blessed that had not happened.

I gathered that Kaylen resolved in her mind not to accept our help before we read our letters. I knew she heard what we said, and to her credit, she never denied that she had a problem with drugs and was addicted; she just didn't want our help. Not at that time, anyway.

Kaylen wanted the help to extend to her marriage and by association her husband. We could not do that. We were there solely for her. It was not a package deal; especially with all the water under the bridge from the past two decades of degenerated debauchery. So, Kaylen in her fierce head-strong manner, jacked up on heroin, left our presence that day with the thought that she could manage and handle her addicted lifestyle herself and restore her relationship with Kyle.

While we had not come away with everything we wanted, the mission was well executed with a two-way track of truth. The intervention team had done its' level best, and as hockey parents say to their kiddos after a tough game, we "left it all on the ice." We each spoke our truth and heard each other's words, including Kaylen.

On that fresh new morning of living my truth, I reflected with gratitude on the bittersweet moments that surfaced through the intervention. There had been a unity in the hodge-podge of people that came together as a family to loosen the grip of addiction on Kaylen, even if it had been like herding cats to assemble us together. John was an earthly angel that had come into our lives and had brought some semblance of sense to the chaos for my aged parents, especially when mom's financial enabling weakness had been revealed. John bridged the gap of my dad's anger and disappointment at the situation in a respectful peer-centered way that no one else could have done. Chris played full out. He said and did what only he could in the moments with Kaylen, Julee, and our parents. All of it, every moment, every word, every tear and every deed had been an act of love; a great vortex of love. Love for each other, love for family of origin, and for family of choice, and love for a person suffering from addiction. I was at peace knowing that truth was spoken that day and that each of us did all that we were capable of doing. I wrote a poem that morning and texted it to Kaylen.

An Odd Cleanse

Truth was in the room
As pain in our hearts loom
Like heavy clouds that fog the view
We were all there, prepared and on queue
Hopeful spirit within our midst
And still lingers in this morning's mist
A raw, cold snow/rain mix
That speaks the heart
That the seeds we planted will germinate and start.

With this new peculiar energy that I embodied as faith, I did something new, something I had never done before. I planted flowers from seeds as an act of devotion to love Kaylen from afar with recovery in mind. I chose to plant sunflowers, as those were Aunt Chrissie's favorite.

I had never planted anything from seed before and knew next to nothing about that method of gardening. In the past, I had bought flowers from the local greenhouse or the store when they were on sale. Like an elementary school science project, I started the seeds in little paper cups. I hydrated the dirt, measured it, placed the seeds and covered the seeds with more soil. I called these little guys my "seeds of recovery" and checked on them each day. And what do you know, they grew! Not straight stalk picture perfect, but they grew nonetheless. When summer reached its' peak, I transplanted the sunflower starts to the front garden box Chris had built with our son the year before as a Mother's Day gift. And like the fidelity present in the intervention process, my sunflower seeds of recovery grew wildly.

10

Birds of a Feather

I GAZED OUT THE OVAL WINDOW OF THE 747, ready for takeoff, and I imagined the words we had spoken to Kaylen at the intervention as deeply embedded truth seeds that would germinate in her soul. I was on a plane to meet up with mom and a friend of hers that had invited me to visit Las Vegas with them. This long weekender was the best non-decision, along-for-the-ride choice I ever made, and it happened to fall on the weekend after Kaylen's intervention. A value-added bonus of this trip was that a lifelong soul sister girlfriend of mine lived in Las Vegas.

As the plane departed and Anchorage's cityscape coastline evaporated into the clouds, I prayed the words we spoke resonated and rooted somewhere inside Kaylen's ever-eclipsing spirit. I imagined that our statements wrapped around her like a warm, beloved childhood blanket fresh from the dryer that protected her as she ran the cold harsh streets of Anchorage in active addiction. I visualized our testaments to her replaying in her mind like a game film an athlete reviews that reveals missteps that could improve how she played the game of life. I hoped that intervention moments cycled in her psyche as a perpetual reminder that she was a loved member of our family, that we could do this, that she could do this, and that we were there to help and support her. I departed Alaska at peace, knowing that our collective heartfelt devotions were released on Kaylen.

The first day in Vegas was surreal. It felt like I landed in a different world by way of escape pod into a childlike adult happy fun land. My delicate, emotionally wiped out self, walked dazed and confused into a hoochie momma environment of forced merriment. Mom was a brittle shell of herself amidst the over-stimulating surround sound and blinking bright lights of the casinos. The great effort and strong united presence at the intervention appeared to have shrunk mom by three inches.

Like a teacher with school children on a field trip, mom's friend Shelby shepherded us around Las Vegas to meals, the pool, live music performances and silly happenings on the strip that reminded us of the goofiness of life. We dressed up in nice clothes, went out for yummy food, saw shows and did activities that distracted our attention from the uncertainty and turmoil of Kaylen's addiction. It felt good to be in a cheery, warm and bright place and not in our shields up, reactionary crisis mode. Smiles appeared on our faces as we allowed ourselves to enjoy fun moments with each other. In this space, time zones away from home, I discovered the depth and breadth of the mental time and energy my sister's active addiction had been taking.

It was a priority for me and Stephanie to connect while I was in Las Vegas. Stephanie and I have known each other since high school. She moved to Las Vegas several years ago for a job with benefits, a type of employment that is hard to come by in Alaska. We've been friends through a lot of life stuff, including becoming mothers, marriages, divorces, raising children, parenting and relationship betrayals, along with health and work issues. Stephanie is the type of girlfriend that you do not have to talk to or be with all the time. Conversations and time with Stephanie start where we are in life, and if you are in striking distance of her physical location, someway, somehow Stephanie will connect with you. Stephanie also has a sixth sense to know when and how to show up in life's sticky moments. Stephanie will find a way to show up and grace your life in just the right way and, without fail, she has the best prayer for any situation.

Stephanie picked me up from the hotel in her zippy little fuel efficient car. She wore *Vogue*-ish sunglasses that accentuated her beautiful long grey hair tussled from the car windows being down. She parked at the hotel entrance, ran over, and two-arm-chest-to-chest hugged me like girlfriends do when they haven't seen each other for a while.

Once in the car, Stephanie spouted off a list of activities we could do in the time we had together. We decided to go to the Hoover Dam so we could talk on the drive.

"Tell me everything," she said.

I downloaded the details of the intervention and the extent of the emotional, financial, and time outlay each of us had devoted to the effort and the collective disappointment that Kaylen did not immediately accept the help we offered. I released the mixed sentiments of grief with peace and vulnerable truth that was exchanged while Kaylen chose to be out there reeling in her addiction. Stephanie nodded with "uh-huhs," "okays," and a couple of, "oh mys," as she graciously held non-judgmental space for me.

We stopped at what Stephanie called a healthy fast-food burger place for takeout to eat on the drive. Stephanie dashed into the restaurant to get our food while I waited by the car and absorbed vitamin D from the fully exposed sun pouring over my depleted body like a honey spa treatment. I squeezed every ounce of goodness out of this quiet alone moment and intentionally positioned my face towards the bright sun. Like a well-trained yoga instructor, the sun kinesthetically cued release of my tense body from head to toes. I leaned against my bestie's car in a state of calm and harmony with the universe, knowing that I had done all I could with all the people that I love. I did my level best and spoke truth to my sister, my mom was safe with her friend at the hotel, my kids were secure at school, and my husband and dad were doing what guys do when their wives are out of state on a girlfriend trip. It dawned on me that I was alone for the first time in a long time, and I was calm.

That quiet solitary moment dashed when I heard my phone. It was a call from Shelby. *She's probably calling with mom questions about the time and location of tonight's dinner*, I thought to myself. I answered, "Hey there, how are you two doing this fine day? Having fun? You two behaving?"

"Michaela, your mom got a text notification from a bank to confirm withdrawal from your family's investment account! She didn't know if the text was real or fake so she showed it to me! We called the number on the text and they won't help because your mom doesn't know about the account, the passwords, or security questions! We called your dad and there's no answer!" Shelby frantically recapped.

My heart and shoulders sank further as if another torpedo was shot at this sinking ship I was on. *Here we go again*, I thought to myself. *The one time I leave my mom and this happens. Another direct hit with tidal wave after-effects that crash down on my mom and after-shock waves that ripple through our family, friends, and community. Now I know why Kaylen kept asking for our uncle's birthday and middle name.* I could hear mom's tearful confusion in the background over Shelby's anxious deep breaths. Mom got on the phone.

"Why would Kaylen do this to us, Michaela? Does she not like us?" Mom tearfully pled.

"Mom, this is the addiction, not the Kaylen we know, not our Kaylen," I disquietly responded.

Mom quickly reverted to snarkiness and snapped a harsh remark into the phone, something along the lines of, "That's easy for you to say," or "Nice excuse for her to steal from her family!"

I retracted my head and body from the phone; a physical reaction to get away from this shit! *I'm not doing this anymore*, I thought to myself. *I am miles away and there is nothing I can do. Mom has to sit with her feelings about what is happening without me. Dad has to do something himself. This is not my problem. I am not meant to be with either one of them at this moment. I am meant to be away from them.* Somehow I got off the phone with my mother.

Stephanie returned to the car with our lunch and instantly knew by the look on my face that something had transpired in the fifteen minutes that had elapsed.

"What happened?" Stephanie asked.

"I just got off the phone with mom. Someone's trying to withdraw money from my parents' investment account," I said.

"Oh dear, I'm so sorry this happening to your family. What can we do?" Stephanie asked.

"Nothing! There is nothing I can do! The one day I'm away from this shit and it still finds me!" I bawled.

"Do you still want to go to the Hoover Dam?" Stephanie gently asked.

"Absolutely! I want to get as far away from this shit as I can," I said.

And with that she handed me lunch, got in the car, put it in gear, and drove. *Here I am on my way to the Hoover Dam, caught up in another crisis of my sister's making.* I began a verbal vent session to Stephanie. "So basically my sister is stealing tens of thousands of dollars from the family as we speak and there is nothing that can be done about it. That's what's going on, right now. Incredible," I exclaimed.

My insides churned with big emotions of despair and anger. And just like that, I was emotionally exhausted again. This latest crisis had stolen all of the sunshine energy that had been poured into me just moments before.

This latest crisis was a bit of a bubble-popper, to say the least, which required me to force enjoyment of the monumental man-made construction of the Hoover Dam. I speed read the tourist information placards that the Hoover Dam had been built during the Great Depression and sat upon two time zones. *How apt,* I thought, *I'm depressed and feeling lost in space and between time zones right about now.*

My phone vibrated. It was dad. "Michaela! Where are you? Are you with mom?" Dad barked.

"No, I'm at the Hoover Dam with Stephanie. Did mom get a hold of you about the withdrawal notification on her phone?" I asked.

"Yes! Yes!! It's Kaylen! I need you to wah, wah, wah . . . ."

The directives dad shot my way from the voice squawk box in my hand glanced by my ears like arrows through the air waves as I simultaneously stood and drifted away from Earth with one foot in Nevada and one in Arizona. While dad continued to holler "to-do" items and "I needs," a large black bird with a spot of orange appeared in my visual frame against the white cement back-drop of the dam, and like a bullet, dove into the deep blue pooled water before me. I recognized the bird as a cormorant. I waited to see if the cormorant would pop up from its deep dive. *Nothing. Maybe I missed it,* I thought to myself.

My grandmother had always said that birds were heaven-sent messengers. That day as I stood in two different states both literally and figuratively, the universe signaled to me that Kaylen dove deeper into her addiction; that her rock bottom was below sea level and our family would enter a new level of Depression-era history.

In hindsight, this post-intervention venture afforded the ideal amount of time, space, and distance to detach from my parents and decompress from the emotional outlay from the previous week's events. I stood firm and disconnected from my sister's madness, mom's despair, dad's brusqueness, husband's wariness, children's faltering faith, and the helplessness of the situation. I prayed that the caring cloak we had delivered to Kaylen at intervention protected her like coastal state waters do the cormorant species.

"Dad, I can't do any of that right now. I'm not at a computer and don't have that with me. You'll have to do this yourself," I said into the phone's speaker.

"I understand. Take care of your mother." Dad hung up the phone. Addiction 4, Kelleyburys 1.

11

God Bless Aunt Mary

AFTER THE INTERVENTION, thick fortified walls formed on the outside of me to protect from Kaylen's rejection of our help and accept the reality of her condition. I collected all the broken pieces of my heart and stuffed them deep down so I could get out of the house each day without crying. I was torn up with feelings of anger and sadness that Kaylen had succumbed to such depths. My mind understood that Kaylen's dependency on drugs was severe, while my heart felt that she chose drugs and those people over her family.

After several months, I conditioned myself with steeled armor to attend social gatherings. I compartmentalized the fact that Kaylen was unthinkingly lost and enslaved to a dark underworld. I was matter of fact when friends asked about Kaylen. I responded with curt responses of "not good" or "last I knew she was still alive." These abrupt answers generally led to an awkward silence. I had no nice, pre-packaged words for the black hole my sister was sucked into. Behind my terse responses was a well of troubled tears infused with mental images of the worst that could happen to my sister. An ocean of emotion welled deep within me. I was a puddled mess on the inside while trying to be a normal adult person on the outside. I wasn't doing too good even though I meditated and walked my dogs daily, saw a counselor weekly, went to the gym bi-weekly, and did all the things I could do to divert the hamster wheel of mental energy from the harsh reality that a person I had loved, for a lifetime, was hanging out at the fringes of hell.

My anger, sadness, and disappointment reached a fatigued plateau. I transited through life at a distance with despondent thinking loops that Kaylen was alone and unsafe in a cold corner of hell hustling her way to the next fix by any means necessary. Graphic story lines of her savage and desperate survival on the cold streets of Anchorage replayed like a drive-in movie in the back of my mind. These mental videos played on an endless loop that distracted my mindful presence at my day job with co-workers, clients, my husband, children, friends, aunties, uncles, and parents.

I trained myself to put a fake focus on the positive. I put my mind on what was good in each moment. When friends asked how it was going, my prepared response was, I'm okay, the kids are good and healthy.

I was not living or speaking my truth, and everyone knew it. I wasn't okay. It must have been awkward and annoying to my still uncomfortable but genuinely concerned friends. The struggle is real when there is a not equal sign between the internal self and the outside world.

My conversations with others pinged from a hopelessly heavy heart to short quips to protect myself from pricking the membrane of sad, suppressed sentiment that brimmed within me. My presence was empty, as my soul was preoccupied with Kaylen reeling in an underworld of addiction and the fact that there was nothing I could do about it. I was helpless, hopeless, and becoming resigned that this was it. This was how my sister's life would end and it would be a sad, dark chapter in the lives of my parents, children, our extended family and the community. How would I carry this cross?

By mid-summer, Aunt Mary flew to Alaska and stayed a couple months as a house guest. Mary is one of my dad's seven sisters; and our oldest living auntie. Aunt Mary is a free spirit vegan; the type of woman who seems like she is in motion even when she's not. She is an open minded, self-taught artist and independent thinker. Back in the day, Aunt Mary worked as a journalist, ran for mayor of the small West Virginia town where she raised her two sons and built her own ex-pat bungalow on the island of Nevis. She is the mother of two adult sons, my cousins, as well as a grandmother and a godmother a couple times over. Aunt Mary stands tall, thin, fair skinned with long grey hair, and airy blue eyes.

Mary's arrival to Alaska was light and a breath of fresh air in that prolonged, cold grey winter that had ravaged our family. We caught up on each other's lives, kids, health, and the overall state of our family's union. Midway through one of our catch-up conversations, Mary said, "I want to see my niece."

The late evening Alaskan summer sun beamed through the glass of water on the dining table and onto her lithe, cancer surviving frame like a warrior angel called for duty. Her buoyant blue eyes turned to steel that looked directly into the innards of my soul. I could not resist the direct reach of her stare. I wanted to close my eyes to block her truth speak from penetrating the truth well within me. Her resolute and uncompromising tone took me back to when I was her flower girl and she directed me to be in a certain place and do a certain thing.

I did not want to return to the shadowy world of addiction. I had worked so hard to distance myself from that base biosphere. I worked so hard to brace myself for these discussion ramps with a clenched jaw and rigidly braced shoulders. I could not avoid Mary's directness with weak excuses.

"Mary, it's been several months since I've seen Kaylen. The last time I saw her was at the intervention we did in April. I have no idea where Kaylen is and don't know where to begin to look for her in the drug world," I said.

Kaylen hadn't posted on social media for months, and the only indications that she was alive were police blotters of her arrests that pinged on my phone. In her delicate yet dogged manner, Mary maintained her position with curious prompts and questions about Kaylen's husband, her friends, and other possible starting points to locate Kaylen. I maintained my distance, advising Mary of the boundaries we had set at the intervention. Mary rounded out her soft cross examination of me with direct facts that she had travelled from Georgia, and it was unlikely that she would be this close in geographic proximity to Kaylen ever again.

In loving service to my beautiful Auntie, I called Julee to find Kaylen. Julee kept in touch with Kaylen and told me that last she knew, Kaylen and Kyle were at a hotel in the squalid part of town. My heart and shoulders sank with the knowledge that the floor of Kaylen's rock bottom had fallen out beyond basement level to the point of way below sea level. My sister and brother-in-law were homeless, staying at the skankiest, most dirty, bed bug-infested no-tell-motel in town, and my Aunt Mary wanted to go there. And just like that, the demon of addiction returned to the front steps of my heart and the forefront of my mind, championed by my own Aunt Mary.

I drove to the no-tell-motel with Aunt Mary riding shotgun and circled the building's perimeter. Pale, scabby women with bruised arms and legs dribbled out of the front door of the motel with their bags and backpacks stuffed with all their worldly belongings to aimlessly stroll the sidewalk. A parade of young adults vacuously trolled the back alleys like barely existing zombies. Small clusters of hoodie wearing people huddled in groups at far corners of vacant fenced parking lots marked with no trespassing signs. Tinted window vehicles lapped the motel block in sync with the checkout time to meet their target market and capitalize on the cravings of the drug dependent users that exited their previous night's shelter.

I pulled into a parking area of the worn, outdated, two story blueish-gray motel. The windows were covered in cheap, brightly colored blankets. My hockey mom stickered car stuck out like a bright orange star fish on a black sand beach. The tinted up low rider cars slowly drove by me. A tense, uneasy feeling of being sized up by the shadowy presence inside those rolling vessels that assessed my wide-eyed presence that simultaneously disallowed my sight of them churned my stomach. I didn't need to see them. I could feel the heavy dark energy that oozed like tar from that city block. I considered that the players in this black market and those that profit and feed off them noted details of my car and what I looked like to deduce connections and exploit that information.

Mary and I texted the last numbers we had for Kaylen and waited for a response. Then, without a word, Mary stepped out of the car and walked to the northeast corner of the parking lot to stand by the pale, scabby women. Mary took stock of the space, expanded her energy, and shined brightly at the street corner like the distinguished warrior that she was in that moment in the most bleak and shadowy of places. Mary's light radiated like a lighthouse on that cold, dewy morning. Her grace and unconditional love for humanity gleamed like the Alaska summer sun and dissipated the fog of hopelessness that had amassed within me.

Then, from the corner of my eye, I recognized the stride and body type of a tall, thirty-something man in sneakers without socks, donning a long-sleeved hoodie and below the knee shorts lope into my frame of vision. I quickly rolled down the window to yell at him. He stopped, looked over, and recognized me. It was Kyle. We tentatively walked toward each other. The closer we got, the more I could see his gaunt, sallow being. His pocked face was covered with stubble and his signature basketball shorts revealed scabs and bruises on his legs. I wanted to hug him, but for a myriad of reasons couldn't and wouldn't. Fortunately, he spoke first.

"Hey, how are you?" he asked.

"I'm looking for Kaylen, do you know where she is?" I pointedly asked.

"She's in Chugiak right now," Kyle responded.

Aunt Mary walked toward us.

"How are you, Kyle?" I asked, biding time until Mary joined us.

"I'm doing okay under the circumstances," he said. "How are the kids?"

My heart melted as this genuine human quality surfaced. He knows my children are my life and seemed sincerely interested.

"They're doing good Kyle, thanks for asking. We all miss Kaylen. Do you know how I can get ahold of her? Aunt Mary is in town and wants to see her."

Mary then joined us.

"Yeah, I got calls from a number I didn't recognize," he said curiously.

"It was probably Mary; she really wants to see her niece. Kyle, this is Aunt Mary."

"I figured," he said, "you all look alike. It's nice to meet you."

"It's nice to meet you, too," Mary said. "I'm sorry I was unable to make it to the wedding. Can you connect me with Kaylen; I'd really like to see her while I'm here in Alaska. I've travelled a long way."

"I don't know what time she'll be back. I can get a message to her and maybe you can connect tomorrow," Kyle suggested.

"That'd be great, what time tomorrow? We'll be here," Mary said definitively.

"Tomorrow morning at 10 a.m."

"Thank you," Mary said, "you have my number and we have yours. We'll see you tomorrow morning. I'm going to go sit in the car, I'm cold. It was nice to meet you, Kyle."

And with that Mary left the conversation and went to the car.

I thanked Kyle and passed on that his grandmother had reached out to me and that she was concerned about him. As he walked away, he replied over his shoulder that he called them, and he'd see me tomorrow. I watched Kyle walk towards another part of town. I returned to the car and sat with Mary in awe of what had just occurred. For Kyle to appear at that moment in time, enter my field of vision, and that I recognized him in the condition he was in was mind-blowing. Mary and I drove away from the motel, made a healthy dinner and went to bed early to get a good night's sleep and to prepare for the next day's encounter with Kyle and hopefully Kaylen. Addiction 4, Kelleyburys 2.

12

Eighty-Sixed From a One Star Motel

IT WAS ANOTHER COLD, RAINY, GREY ALASKA MORNING. Mary was up, bright-eyed-and-bushy-tailed, ready to meet with Kyle and hopefully connect with Kaylen. We got in the car, sat and paused to contemplate what we were doing before we launched. Mary questioned whether Kyle would keep his word and appear. I also considered whether Kyle would show up since there were so many times in the past he had not. The difference this time was that I now knew why he didn't show up and that truth was out there for all to see. Mary and I discussed whether we could trust Kyle.

Trust is a nebulous concept in addiction. By the time I appeared at the ragged motel, Kaylen and Kyle had already supplied access to our childhood home to druggie drudges that robbed our parents' house, and someone who had access to my parents' financial documents tried to withdraw funds from their investment account. I didn't know if Kaylen and Kyle knew that stuff was stolen from our parents' house or about the attempt that was made to withdraw funds. I didn't know whether they were involved in some way or if there was some sort of tally that Kaylen and Kyle had with others in the drug world. I didn't know if a drug king pin or fellow junkie felt wronged or owed something. I was uncertain whether Kaylen and Kyle were being used as pawns, whether they were together, or even trusted or loved each other anymore. There was so much water under that bridge that it crossed my mind that this meet up could be a set up to acquire more information for exploitation purposes.

As we approached the hotel city block to meet Kyle my hands gripped the steering wheel in white knuckle style, chest and shoulders became heavier and tighter, teeth clenched and nerves amped with anxiety. Mary texted Kyle and he responded to drive to the back-alley parking lot and follow him. There he stood on the worn asphalt backstreet wearing his beloved Seahawk hoodie and knee length shorts that matched. He directed us to the parking lot on the backside of the hotel. Mary and I texted and called the last known numbers we had for Kaylen.

A second-floor window covering was pulled back and quickly released when we glanced at the movement in that direction. Cryptic text communication from Kaylen pinged on our phones that if the family cut her off, then she cuts the family off. Mary and I tried to decipher Kaylen's communication and responded that Aunt Mary was in town and wanted to see her. Kaylen responded that we did not understand what she had to do to have shelter for the night. Mary maintained text communication with Kaylen and encouraged her to come out of the motel.

Mary and I were parked in the motel parking lot for several hours and stared at the second-floor window and doors with hope that Kaylen would make her way out to see Mary. Kaylen never did come out of the motel that morning, and with heavy hearts Mary and I decided to leave. I drove to a small town that hosted a summer festival. I thought it would be a nice distraction from the cold reality of Kaylen's harsh rejection of us to attend the fair and look at some locally crafted art. The small town is an hour's drive south of Anchorage on Alaska's one highway that buttresses mountains on the left and a water view on the right. The surround sound feel of Mother Nature's grounding and cleansing natural environment calmed, soothed, and comforted our wracked systems after our failed efforts to connect with Kaylen. As we drove further south, the temperature dropped, and the weather changed to hard rain.

It was too cold and wet to walk about the fair to see the artisans' crafts and vendors' wares, and we were drained, cold, and hungry. We had lunch at a café in the mountain ski resort hotel. Over a comfort food-fueled lunch of herbal tea, tomato soup, and shared side of grilled Brussels sprouts, we released the fretful energy that our connection with Kyle conjured and let down the sad reality that we were unsuccessful in coaxing Kaylen out of the motel. We reflected on the morning's events and tried to make sense of Kaylen's words. We were at peace knowing we had done all we could and were grateful for the connections we did make with Kyle and Kaylen, even if superficially unfruitful.

After lunch, we drove home to rest from the emotionally draining and eventful day. It was still raining, and the clouds hung low, cold and heavy like our hopes. As we approached the uphill section that ascends into Anchorage, windshield wipers slapping, I answered a call from my dad.

"Hey dad, you're on speaker, Mary and I are in the car driving back from having lunch in Girdwood. What's up?" I hollered in the phone over the loud pouring rain.

"Yeah, Michaela here's the situation," dad commenced his signature directive tone. "Your sister Kaylen called and asked for help. She knows the rule that I'll help with the money end of things if she goes to treatment. Apparently, she's on board with that and needs a place to stay until we can get her into treatment. Can you get her a place to stay? I'll pay you back."

"Omigosh, dad we're pulling into Anchorage now. Mary and I spent the morning trying to get Kaylen to be with us and she wanted nothing to do with us. Is she really ready, and will she come with us?" I asked.

"Well, apparently with the change in weather she had a change of heart. She has no place to go and says she'll work with the family to get into treatment. Can you get her somewhere? She can't stay here at the house with me and your mother."

"Well, how are we going to do this?" I asked. "She can't stay at my house. That was a boundary Chris and I agreed on because of the kids and I can't stay with her because of the dogs."

"I'll pay for a room somewhere until we can get this treatment thing worked out," dad said.

Mary piped up and said, "I'll stay with her."

"Mary that's nice and generous of you, but I don't want to put that on you or expose you to anything," dad said.

"Lenny, it's okay—I'm a big girl and she's my niece, too. I can stay with my niece at a hotel and be with her," Mary maintained.

"If Kaylen's willing to get treatment she will need to detox and deal with withdrawals. What do we do about that?" I asked.

Mary said that she'd stay with Kaylen while she detoxed and went through withdrawals. Dad wanted to get Kaylen a room for the night and reassess the next day. Dad made it clear that he was only paying for Kaylen, not Kyle. Our conversation ended with some semblance of a plan that Mary and I would pick Kaylen up from the motel and get her a place to stay for the night.

I drove to the motel while Mary texted Kaylen that we were on our way. Mary and I dissected each text received from Kaylen and carefully crafted every text sent to her. Mary texted Kaylen that she would stay with her while we got help for treatment. Kaylen quickly returned Mary's text with, "No thanks!"

Mary maintained text communication with Kaylen while simultaneously confused by the words she texted. We continued to the motel not knowing how we would physically connect with Kaylen. I parked at the motel's front parking area. Mary sent a text to Kaylen telling her our location. I unlocked the car doors, and like a silent car jacker Kaylen undetectably appeared in the back seat of my car.

I hadn't seen Kaylen in months, and I barely recognized her. Her long brown hair was matted, faded, and frizzy. Her skin was pocked and pale, with makeup unevenly splotched on her face. Her tiny frame and face were swollen. She wore several layers of clothes, long sleeve shirts, a hoodie, and ripped designer blue jeans that were now skintight on her. She had a couple of backpacks and purses stuffed and overflowing with who knows what. I locked the car doors, turned my body to the front windshield and talked to her through the rear-view mirror like a parent does with a troubled toddler in the back seat.

"Hello, Kaylen," I said to her looking from the rear-view mirror.

"Hey, dad said you'd get me a place to stay," Kaylen said without eye contact.

"It's nice to see you. Did you see Aunt Mary's here?" I asked so she would know we were not lying earlier.

"Hey Mary," Kaylen pithily said to Mary.

"Hello Kaylen," Mary said, sizing up Kaylen's presentation.

"Dad said he'd pay for a place for you to stay and that you agreed to treatment. We're here to get a place for you to stay while getting you into treatment," I clarified.

"I'm not going to some fucking Club Med treatment rehab center Sis," Kaylen hissed from the back seat.

I inhaled deeply, clenched my teeth, bit my reactionary tongue and the inside of my cheeks, placed my focus on the present moment that Kaylen was alive and, in my car, and pondered what the next right step was in this semblance of a plan that my dad, Aunt Mary, and I had concocted.

"Let's find a place for right now," I suggested. "Apparently you don't want Aunt Mary staying with you."

"Yeah, no. Thanks, but no thanks. I don't need a fucking baby-sitter. I'm a grown ass adult that can take care of myself, thank you very much," she insolently jeered from the back seat.

I was insulted by the audacity of her brash claim that she had the ability to take care of herself when clearly, she could not. *She has no job, no money and looks like shit. Obviously, she cannot care for herself.* But I did not say any of that. She was completely oblivious to the irony and factual inaccuracy of her ungrateful and hostile tone and words. It took every fiber of my being not to state the obvious to her, but where would that get me? What dignity would that bestow? None, and I might lose her. I continued to take deep breaths to maintain composure and not unleash that we were there to pick her ass up because she was a fucking homeless junkie! In effort to impart upon her some control in a world where she had none, I asked her where we should go for a place for her to stay.

She softened a bit and said, "Well, my stuff is here so, here?"

"You want to stay here?" I incredulously asked her.

Still communicating through the rear-view mirror, she mutely nodded yes.

"Let's see what is available," I said.

I parked the car to face the roadway, left it running with heat for Mary and entered the hotel with Kaylen.

In my thirty-five-plus years of living in this town of two hundred and fifty thousand people, I never stepped foot inside this particular motel due to its reputation. The depth of my sister's addiction had to be pretty bad to be at a place where the local news regularly reports people dying from gun violence. With Kaylen beside me, I opened the front glass door and walked into the dimly lit foyer. The space was stale and had stained, well-tread, blood red carpets with cheap, dark wood paneled walls. We positioned ourselves at the front desk and asked the clerk for a room. The large, portly thirty-something Caucasian man behind the desk asked for my identification and credit card, none of which I felt comfortable giving him. I explained that I would not be staying in the room and that the room was for my sister. I offered to pay cash, so my credit card and identification were unnecessary. The burly, yellow-stained t-shirted man said the hotel's policy required an ID of the person who would be staying in the room. I looked to my sister.

Kaylen whispered my direction, "I don't have my ID."

I whispered back, "Where is it?"

"I don't know. Maybe Kyle has it," she said in a low tone.

"Why would Kyle have your ID?" I softly asked her.

"Maybe because I'm married to him," she responded in her smart-ass way.

The man behind the desk overheard our whispered conversation and blurted, "Wait, I recognize you. You're married to Kyle. That guy is **eighty-sixed** from here. You can't stay here."

Kaylen snapped back at the clerk, "You're refusing service to me because of who I'm married to?"

There I stood in the dank, sparse lobby in shock, and utter disbelief that my sister was refused service from the most vile and squalliest no-tell-motel in the foulest part of town and was arguing with the clerk about it. I felt I was on Willy Wonka's scary boat ride and wondered how I got here. I ushered Kaylen away from the clerk's desk to a dark corner of the motels tiny lobby next to vending machines of over-priced cigarettes, chocolate bars, and caffeinated drinks to problem solve with her.

"Kaylen, they're not gonna let you stay here. What are we going to do?" I asked.

"All my stuff and dog are here," she disclosed.

"Your dog is here? Where?" I asked.

"Around the corner," she said. And like a light bulb went off in her head she announced, "I know! There's a place nearby we can try."

We left the dank motel to get in the car with Aunt Mary, who was still sitting in the front passenger seat, and drove the back alleys to another motel one block over. While in transit, I briefed Mary on the happenings and drove past Kaylen's dog chained to a wooden electrical pole. I pulled up to the front of a two-and-a-half story, light brown log façade motel. My sister and I got out of the car and stepped up into the brightly lit motel lobby to the front desk. I asked the elderly Korean man for a room. I told him that the room was for my sister and that I would pay cash. The man and his wife indicated availability on the second floor for one person, no dogs. I said we'd take it and filled out the paperwork while my sister plopped herself into a big brown leather couch that faced a locked television cabinet in the motel's lobby and used my phone to send texts.

After I completed the paperwork, the small Korean woman led us to the second-floor room by way of a cramped, well-lit stairwell and proudly showed us the room. My sister rummaged about the room, opened drawers and inspected the bathroom. When the manager had left the room, my sister fell backwards spread eagle with a big, content-ed smile on her face onto the motel's double bed as if she owned the space. I asked my sister if she was hungry, and like a teenage babysitter I ordered a Canadian bacon with pineapple pizza and root beer for delivery. The pizza arrived quickly, and my sister devoured it like she hadn't eaten in weeks. While my sister ate, I looked at my phone and saw she had texted several numbers that notified her location. I said good night to Kaylen, reminded her of the rules of no dogs and no Kyle, and that dad would be there in the morning to pick her up. Addiction 4, Kelleyburys 3.

13

"Just in Case..."

THE NEXT MORNING MY PHONE RANG. It was dad. His loud voice blared in my ear for all those within his vicinity to hear:

"Yeah, Michaela, I'm here to pick up your sister. She had the dog in the room and it's now in the back of my truck. Kyle is here. The hotel owner says no dogs and wants more money. Don't give him any. Kaylen, you're either coming with me and your dog; or you're going with him. Make your choice."

Long pause. I could hear dad's heavy heart attack-surviving breaths over the phone like he had just finished a marathon, and with a softer tone he continued, "Alllright, ooookay, she put her stuff in the back of the truck, she's coming with us. See you later Michaela, meet you at the office, bye-bye." He hung up.

My phone rang again, this time from an unidentified number. Not knowing if it was Kyle or persons Kaylen had texted the previous night, I answered. It was the Korean motel owner squawking in broken English that more money was due because my sister had a dog in the motel room. I ended that call and shuffled to the shower to get ready for the day and meet up with my dad and sister.

As I made the forty-five-minute drive into town, my mind pondered what my dad and sister were doing. I slowly walked up the stairs to my office, not knowing what to expect when I arrived. The door to our office was uncharacteristically closed. I sensed a contained chaotic energy on the other side of the door. I placed my hand on the knob, inhaled deeply, turned the handle, gradually exhaled, opened the door, and stepped into the office. My curly-haired, red headed assistant was seated at the desk with her ear to the phone. She looked at me with wide eyes and nodded her head in the direction of the etched glass door of the conference room where dad and Kaylen were seated.

My six foot, two hundred pound, seventy-two-year-old father was hunched over the table with his back to me, wearing khaki safari pants with a matching jacket. Yellow legal pad papers were spread all around him. Kaylen was seated next to him at the table in stylish jeans and long-sleeved shirt. Her arms and legs were crossed like a troubled teen, with purses, bags and backpacks at her feet. Her appearance was slightly improved from the day before, probably due to having slept in a bed and not on the streets or holed up in an abandoned car or house.

I walked past the conference room, made eye contact with Kaylen and advanced to my office where that door was closed, too. I opened the door and saw Mary at my desk on her phone, reviewing mail that arrived for her at my office. I wondered, *did dad drive all the way out to his house to drop off Kaylen's dog and bring Mary into town with him? Did Kaylen stay in the truck while at home? Meh, didn't matter. My mind didn't need to go down that rabbit hole. We're all here together and safe right now.*

I put my briefcase and purse down on the chairs in front of my desk and made way to the conference room. I squeezed between the conference room wall and my dad's girth to place myself at the head of the table, across from my sister. I could see dad's copious chicken scratch notes on the crinkled papers in piles that only he could read. I could tell that he had put time and effort into research of transitional housing for Kaylen. By the time I arrived, he had directed my assistant to call places for Kaylen to board until a referral for treatment could be obtained. It was silent in the room and dad was focused on the next steps of the plan that was forming in his mind. Pricking the thick tense energy in the stuffy room, I gently asked, "How are we all doing?"

Dad brusquely barked, "Everything is under control!"

Dad says that when he is nervous, and things aren't within his control. Dad has always lacked the awareness that his oversized blustery mannerisms land harshly on whatever is delicate and fragile in the room. Dad was all business and continued his narrative on the information he had gathered about pay by the week sober housing. My sister sat subdued at the table as our dad and office assistant hollered back and forth to each other about the costs and logistics of housing Kaylen. Dad next informed that we needed to get Kaylen to a doctor for a referral for treatment and "this" needed to be looked at.

Kaylen lifted her arm and revealed a red, PVC pipe sized forearm with black bruises, open oozing wounds and dried blood about the edges. Her petite fingers and hands were puffed up like sausage links, with discolored welts on the front of her hand.

"Oh man, Kaylen. A doctor needs to look at that," I said gently trying to hide that I was grossed out by the site of the wounds on her arm.

"It's fine. I can take care of it myself as long as I have rubbing alcohol and gauze," she snapped.

Without looking at my sister, my dad continued to talk like she was a potted plant in the room, "She needs to see a doctor. Can you get her into a doctor?"

"What about the doctor that treated you for the injuries from the car wreck?" I suggested. "Maybe we can get an appointment at that clinic, and you can see him."

Dad bellowed to my assistant, "Marie, call that doctor that treated Kaylen in the car wreck to get her an appointment."

Marie dutifully called and said the clinic could get her in tomorrow at 10 a.m.

Dad barked, "We'll take it."

Marie yelled back, "They want to know what type of exam it is and whether it includes gynecological."

Without hearing or appreciating that subtle detail, dad hollered, "Yes, set her up for a full physical exam."

Teeming, Kaylen broke her silence, "I'm not having a gynecological exam!"

Dad slammed his hands on the table and thundered, "You are not in control here!"

Kaylen boomed back, "I am in control of my body!"

"Whoa! Whoa! Whoa!" I called to the two of them while standing up and waving my arms like an elementary school crosswalk guard to contain this rapidly spiraling escalation. In that moment, Kaylen's words and manner of expression signaled harm beyond a seventy-year-old white man's comprehension. Dad was frustrated that the forward progression of the plan in his mind was impeded by what he felt was Kaylen's childish stubbornness and he stormed out of the room.

"Kaylen, dad's trying to pave the way for you to get into treatment . . . let's just set an appointment and deal with the details later," I softly said to her.

"Fine. But I'm not doing a gyno. That's not happening," she said, finally making direct eye contact with me.

"Okay, let me check in with dad. Do you need anything? Water, coffee, tea?"

"Coffee would be great. Do you have any snacks, Sis?" she asked like she was the little girl I would pick up from pre-school twenty-five years earlier.

"Let me see what I can find. I'll be back."

I exited the conference room and confirmed that my assistant had set an appointment for a general exam to get my sister a referral to treatment. I moved towards the mini kitchen in the back of the office and walked past my dad, who was pacing like a wolf protecting entry to its den. I made my sister a cup of coffee, and as I rummaged through the cupboards for the first aid kit, discovered a box of granola bars.

I told dad that it might be best for me and Mary to take Kaylen to the medical appointment since we are women. Dad remained focused on getting Kaylen to sign guardian and conservator papers to me and getting her divorced from Kyle.

Feeling that more bricks were dumped into my people pleasing, how can I fix this, I'm responsible for everything life backpack, I told dad, "One step at a time dad. Right now, she's agreeable to treatment. Let's focus on that."

I returned to the conference room with a bottle of water, snacks, and first aid kit and told Kaylen, "Here are some snacks and water. Your coffee is brewing. Let's see what we can do with your arm."

And with a knowing stare Kaylen said, "Thanks, I got it Sis. I know what to do. I know why it is. I've been doing this for a long time."

We silently looked at each other and held that truth between us for a moment.

"Okay, here's the first aid kit, dear, do what you need to do. Let me know how I can help," and I walked out of the room towards my assistant's desk.

"I'm not doing a gyno, Sis," she yelled in my direction as I exited the room.

"That's fine. Let's just get an appointment to get a referral for treatment," I said as I grabbed papers off Marie's desk. "Here, there are some papers for you to sign in the event something happens so the medical people can call me in case of emergency," I relayed to Kaylen authoritatively.

"What papers?" Kaylen asked.

"Power of attorney for medical and release of medical information, that way the doctors can speak with me if something happens to you," I explained.

I placed the papers on the table and slid them her direction. She read the papers, or acted like she read the papers and said, "I remember these when I was in practice. Me signing this doesn't mean that you say what my treatment will be. Me signing this doesn't mean that you're making those decisions for me. I'm capable of making my own decisions, especially with treatment. I worked in this field," she assertively commanded.

"I understand what you're saying Kaylen. This will not be used unless you agree. It allows the doctors to speak with me, and if it is deemed you can't make medical decisions, the power of attorney allows me to make those decisions on your behalf. You and I need to be square on what your treatment intentions are so those can be effectuated for you," I said, looking directly into her eyes.

She signed the papers and reconfirmed, "I'm capable of making my own decisions."

"I know, this is just in case. I'll scan these into our system and fax them to the clinic for tomorrow's appointment," I said to her reassuringly.

I exited the conference room on a cloud, feeling super successful that major points were scored for team rehab and recovery in a brutal capture the flag battle with addiction. Not only did we have Kaylen in our midst, but we had also gotten her a medical appointment, she signed a power of attorney with release of medical information and safe transitional housing was secured. I instructed my assistant to scan the papers into our system like we would for a client and to fax the power of attorney and release of information to the clinic with a cover sheet for tomorrow's appointment, that way they would know that I would be present at the appointment.

I headed to my office where the door was now opened to inform dad and Mary that Kaylen had signed a power of attorney and medical release, and that the appointment was set for tomorrow morning.

"How will she get there?" dad asked.

"Well, I guess I'll take her," I suggested.

"I'll go with you, Michaela," Mary volunteered. "I'll stay at your house tonight and we'll pick her up and take her to the appointment together tomorrow morning."

"I'll give you the information of the guy I've been talking to who rents the place where I paid for her to stay," dad said.

"Sounds like a plan," I confirmed. "If the appointment is at ten, we should be at that place you rented by nine-thirty at the latest, and that means leaving my house by eight-thirtyish tomorrow morning, which actually means leave by eight to take the dogs to doggy day care," I said out loud for Mary to hear.

"No problem," Mary chimed.

"Woohoo! Yeah team! We have a plan. Let's get something to eat. I'm starving!" I said to the group.

Dad, Mary, and Kaylen left for the rental to pay the manager and drop off Kaylen's stuff while I finished up some paperwork at the office. We met for lunch at the only gentrified whole food grocery store in Anchorage, Alaska. My dad's red extended cab pickup truck pulled into the parking lot and parked farthest away from the store's entry as that is dad's way of getting extra exercise in throughout his day.

Mary and Kaylen poured out of the truck smiley and giggling while dad muttered about the $70 he spent on shoes for Kaylen and that if she uses drugs, she will be kicked out of this place, and he'll lose the three hundred some dollars he put down as a deposit for her housing.

As we walked towards the store entry, Mary maintained light conversation about organic food and how it is medicine for any recovery. Kaylen smartly bragged that she was kicked out of this store, which put the rest of us on notice that this establishment might not serve her, and by association exclude us from service too. I thought to myself, *I am at this market at least twice a week, sometimes more and have never seen you here. Who in the actual hell gets kicked out of a whole food market?*

I was disgusted by Kaylen's smug retelling of a story that she made "quite a scene" and yelled "choice words" at store employees. Embarrassed, I tensely entered the store not knowing whether store personnel would stop us at the entry or follow us through the store to escort us out due to a trespass violation by my sister. Fortunately, we were not asked to leave. We got our food from the deli and salad bar, had lunch and sketched out logistics for the next day.

Mary, dad, and I drove to the rental with Kaylen so I would know where to pick her up the next morning. The temporary housing was in a residential area across from an elementary school that had "Drug Free Zone" signs posted to alert of severe penalties for drug offenses within a school zone. I parked in front of the two-story brown house with white trim windows that had a kept yard with several healthy trees. The space dad rented for Kaylen was accessed through a waist high chain link fence on cement path walkway that led to the right side of the house, down a few stairs and into a daylit basement. The space accommodated drug free group living with a shared kitchen, dining, and sitting area, laundry and private double or single rooms for occupants.

The front door of the space opened into a sparingly furnished common area that had a well-used coffee pot, a table with a couple of metal chairs, a brown cloth couch, and large outdated television with a big, dark wood seventies-style coffee table used as a footstool by a fellow male occupant. Kaylen's room was second door on the right, next to the shower bathroom, sparsely furnished with a twin bed, nightstand, and a lamp. I told Kaylen that we would pick her up a little after nine in the morning to get her to her appointment the next morning.

Mary and I left the rental and debriefed on the drive home about the day's happenings. We verbally sketched out the next day's schedule that accounted for getting the dogs to doggy day care, the likelihood that Kaylen would not be ready for the appointment and that we would probably have to get her ready and do the medical check-in paperwork process for her. Mary and I went to bed early for the next day's event. Addiction 4, Kelleyburys 4.

14

Treatment Options

THE NEXT MORNING MARY WAS UP AND READY TO GO, albeit a bit slower likely due to the previous day's energetic and emotional outlay and the fact that she hadn't had her cancer therapies for several weeks. I gathered my two large Irish setter dogs in the back of the car to drive to doggy day care with Mary riding shot gun. I realized I was tense and prayed that the day's tight morning schedule unfolded smoothly.

When we arrived at doggy day care I hopped out of the car, moved towards the hatchback to put the leashes on, and check them in. Mary asked if she could help. I handed Mary Clyde's leash with the thought that he was the less jumpy of the two; even though he is thirty pounds heavier than Bonnie and the larger dog. As I placed the collar and leash on Bonnie, the jumpy sixty-five-pound dog, Clyde, unexpected-ly bolted towards the front door of doggy-day care yanked Mary over a cement parking bumper. Mary yelped, and her delicate frail body was crumpled down on the ground over the hard surfaced curb and asphalt parking lot in a fetal position, writhing and crying in pain.

The doggy day care people rushed out of the building and took the dogs. I helped Mary to the front passenger seat of my car. My mind begged the universe, *Oh dear God, this is awful. This is not a good thing to happen. Please be with me in these moments. Please be with me. Please make Mary be okay.*

I darted into the building to check-in the dogs, returned to the car and Mary said, "let's just go get to Kaylen."

On the drive to Kaylen's sober living place, my prayers amped for Mary and that Kaylen was ready to go for the medical appointment. I parked at the rental, left Mary in the car and sprinted to Kaylen's space. *Amen, prayers answered*, Kaylen was dressed and ready to go. *Thank you, God*. I told Kaylen that Aunt Mary was not doing well because Clyde pulled her to the ground. I did not know how hurt Mary was, but maybe the clinic could check Mary out when we arrived.

At the clinic, Mary sat in the lobby while Kaylen and I went to the front desk to check in and do paperwork. I was flustered because I knew Mary was hurt. I felt that we were behind the clock, and I hoped we could put the wheels in motion for Kaylen to enter treatment. Kaylen started to fill out the papers and asked me questions that she should know about herself; her social security number and other identification information, none of which she had, nor did I know the answers to off the top of my head. Fortunately, I had made copies of her identification information and restlessly supplied that to the front desk check-in girl with copies of the power of attorney and release of information. Like an exasperated teen, Kaylen took the clip board and huffed away to sit down next to Mary to finish filling out the paperwork. An older lady arrived behind the front desk girl and said, "I'll take over from here."

This new lady looked at me and said, "I think I just spoke with your mom."

"You did?" I said with a smile and looked up at her. "And how is mom doing today?"

"She mentioned that that she has two daughters, that one is a lawyer and that they're supposed to be here today. She asked me about the drug treatment rehab program, and I told her the options that are available here," this nice lady quietly said to me in perfect model of respect for others medical privacy.

"Thank you so very much for taking the time to speak with our mom. This has been very hard, especially on her. If mom calls again, which, knowing my mom, that will happen. You can assure her that her daughters arrived safely," I said.

"Actually, I can't say anything to your mom about your sister. She does not hold a release of information and does not have power of attorney. You do," she correctly stated.

"You are absolutely correct. When mom calls again, you *can* tell her that her lawyer daughter arrived with two other women, one of which she introduced to you as her Aunt Mary," I said to her with a knowing reciprocated smile.

"That I *can* do. I'm going to line your sister up with our doctor that oversees the outpatient treatment program," she said as an understanding team player.

"Thank you so very much. That's actually perfect, as my sister is resistant to inpatient treatment. Also, my sister has sores all over her arm from IV drug use that need to be addressed, too."

"Our lead doctor's medical intern will take care of that. Let's get you ladies checked in and up to see the doctor," she replied.

As she gathered the papers I chirpped, "In all this chaos, I missed your name."

"Anne," she said, "I'm the front area manager. When you call, ask for me. Here's my direct line. Someone will be out shortly to lead you all to the evaluation room."

I think we just signed another player onto team rehab and recovery, I said to myself while my insides did a happy dance.

A nurse came to the lobby area and softly called for my sister. All three of us stood up. I took the lead and walked towards the nurse to introduce myself as Kaylen's sister and confirmed that the release of information and power of attorney were in the medical file. The nurse confirmed that it was all in there and led us up a flight stairs. Mary took the elevator. The nurse proceeded down the hall, past grouped together computers and desks. I recognized one of the nurses at the station as someone I went to high school with. We made eye contact and weakly smiled at each other, knowing my presence there was due to acute, unstable, and dire circumstances.

The nurse led us to a comfy warm sitting area with a nice couch, a couple of high back cushy chairs, a faux fireplace, healthy plants, pleasing wall art, and up to date and interesting health magazines. I nervously waited while Mary continued to shift her body in pain from the dog yank incident that had occurred an hour earlier. Mary asked if she could be examined or have x-rays done here.

A young wide-eyed female in scrubs, about the age of my sister, entered the room, introduced herself as the intern assistant and clarified that it was a small exam room. I introduced myself, my sister, and Aunt Mary and clarified that it was my sister who is being seen and we were here to support her. I explained that I held power of attorney and a release of information for my sister. If my sister wanted me in the exam room with her, I would be present to be that support, and if she preferred privacy, I respected that and would wait here. Mary piped up that she would stay in the waiting room where it was warm and cozy and the two of us could go to the exam room with the provider. Kaylen looked at me and nodded to join her in the exam room.

The medical provider led me and Kaylen to a small room. Kaylen sat on the metal cushioned table covered with medical tissue while I sat in a cold metal chair in the corner. The intern stood in front of Kaylen and asked what she could do for her. Kaylen looked at me. I nodded my head to encourage her. With tears in her eyes, Kaylen pulled up her sleeves to reveal the sores on her arm. I softly said, "My sister is here for help."

With appreciation for what was not said, the intern gently put gloves on to examine and tend to the wounds on Kaylen's arm. She cleaned, bandaged, and wrapped the wounds on Kaylen's arm and explained the different types of treatment options available. Kaylen opened up and softened a bit to absorb the options the intern provided that were available at the clinic. With confidence, Kaylen inserted into the conversation that she was a licensed counselor and had knowledge of inpatient facilities, a clear signal of her resistance to that form of treatment. The medication form of treatment was of interest to Kaylen so that she could return to the job market and a normal life.

The intern and Kaylen talked about the difference between **suboxone** and **methadone**. I was resistant to **narcotic** medication as a treatment method to treat drug addiction, as it didn't make sense to me to treat drug addiction with more drugs. Kaylen would never get clean if she was always dependent on drugs to manage and get through life. I asked the intern what she recommended. The intern graciously explained how the treatment was delivered, the known side effects and rounded out her explanation with, "How about this, I'll get you the information on each of these outpatient treatment options for you to take with you. Review the materials and do your own research to make a decision."

As the intern exited the room, she tenderly placed her hand on Kaylen's shoulder and said, "I know this was hard. I'm proud of you."

Addiction 4, Kelleybury's 5, and a little-known fact about walk-on player to team Kelleybury, St. Anne is the patron saint of mothers and protector of storms.

15

Relapse on the Road to Rehab

WITHIN TWO WEEKS KAYLEN WAS KICKED OUT of the sober living house dad had secured for her. Kyle had entered Kaylen's ground level living quarters through the window, and the manager did not tolerate other people sleeping in the single room. Fortunately, Julee and her husband allowed Kaylen to stay with them at their house. Julee provided updates about Kaylen and reported that Kaylen was content at her home doing simple domestic tasks of laundry, meal preparation, setting the table for meals with others, and being in a family-friendly healthy living environment.

Julee noticed the wounds on Kaylen's arms had become grossly infected and drove Kaylen to the hospital emergency room. Julee sent me a text that Kaylen told the emergency room physician that she was an **IV** drug user and needed help. I seized on this medical encounter and immediately faxed the power of attorney and release of information to the hospital and hoped the emergency room physician would issue a direct referral to the hospital's rehab program without Kaylen being placed on a waiting list. It worked like a charm. In a couple of hours, the hospital's rehab program called to schedule an assessment of Kaylen.

Kaylen detoxed and went through withdrawals at Julee's house. That was the longest weekend of our lives. The following week, Kaylen was admitted to the hospital's intensive multi-week outpatient rehab program for severe substance dependency disorder. Kaylen stayed at Julee's house while she attended the intensive outpatient program.

I became our family's primary contact with Kaylen. I met with our parents weekly to discuss Kaylen's progress in her treatment. The weekly dinner meetings with my parents allowed us to regroup about Kaylen's progress; to collaborate and support each other. Like any good team, where one was weak, others showed up strong. These meetings allowed us to be hopeful and encouraged by advances made, yet tired, sad, weary, disappointed, angry, and hopeless at addiction's continued grip on and possession of Kaylen.

That was how I looked at addiction; a possession of Kaylen that required an exorcism of sorts. I knew Kaylen was in there. We just had to get to her and consistently show up for her with unconditional love. But only to a point though; that is a lesson I learned later. It is a pinball journey running alongside an addict in the arcade game of their existence. It is hard to show up in love for someone with severe drug dependency when the demons of addiction lay in wait at every twist and turn on the road to recovery.

At the weekly dinner meeting with my parents, discussion of Kaylen's admittance to treatment felt like a huge win. We discussed Kaylen's need for transportation and options of a bus pass or Uber fare cards. My parents supplied financial support to Julee for what they called "the proper care and feeding of Kaylen." We agreed that discussion of Kaylen's employment status was on hold since it was Kaylen's full-time job to get clean. Employment efforts had to be on hold while she was in treatment. My dad maintained a focus on getting Kaylen to sign divorce papers.

It felt like Kaylen's treatment for drug addiction was moving in the right direction. Kaylen was in rehab and in a safe place with Julee. With funds supplied by dad, I opened an account I designated as "Kaylen's conservator account." I wrote a contract, which Kaylen signed, with terms for the housing subsidy that included continued rehab treatment and regular **UAs**. Matters with Kaylen felt stable. There was some breathing room. I could take a breath.

I left town to move my daughter into her dorm at school. I received a call from an area code I recognized and answered. It was Kaylen's outpatient rehab therapist. "Kaylen relapsed," she said.

My vision field eclipsed like a toy kaleidoscope that swirled long, narrow and then close up to black. My knees buckled. Instinctively my knees locked back into place in sync with my jaw as I stood at the cashier stand of the big box store with a plastic wand in hand to sign the credit card pad for my daughter's dorm room supplies. The plump cashier stared at me with her big brown eyes to complete the transaction. Her standard issue blue vest and long black hair served as a visual anchor for the disembodied experience I was having. The glaring store lights were headache bright over the long line of parents with carts stuffed full of comforters, pillows, rugs, and extension cords.

What the fuck? I thought to myself. *I'm in another state moving my daughter into school. I can't leave for one week to live and enjoy a moment of my life without Kaylen fucking it up! Can't she just fall in line, do the right thing, and get better?*

"How, how do you know?" stumbled out of my mouth, not wanting to believe the caller and wanting so desperately to believe in my sister.

"We do UAs every day and hers came back positive today. This is actually a good sign. Relapse is part of recovery," the rehab counselor said reassuringly.

"Mom, are you okay?" I heard from my daughter at the end of the check stand behind a pile of pale-yellow pillowcase covers, sheets, and boxes of white wire picture hanging lights.

She looked at me with concern and her voice was the only musical sunshine my ears wanted to hear in that moment. *I'm so sorry sweetheart that you have to deal with this shit. I'm so sorry I am yanked out of 'us' moments,* I telepathically relayed as I stared wide-eyed into her big, green, growing up too fast teenage eyes.

"I have to take this call sweetie; can you finish this?" I said to my daughter, holding back tears of guilt that her auntie had stolen yet another pure positive moment from us.

Fatigued with Kaylen and Kyle's constant crises, my daughter understandingly took the reins of the dorm room move in moment so that I could step aside and into the turn of events that Kaylen's existence currently generated. My phone beeped again; this time it was Kaylen. I told the rehab counselor that Kaylen was on the other line and that I would call her after I got a handle of what was going on with Kaylen. I answered Kaylen's call.

"Sis, I'm checking out of the rehab program. The counselors and therapists don't know what they're doing. They are always picking on me. I'm a therapist and I've worked in outpatient and inpatient clinics, and this is not how it's done. They are violating HIPAA and there's just a lot of stuff I need to do."

I couldn't and wasn't going to argue with Kaylen. I knew nothing about rehab, the nature of her experience, or counseling in a therapeutic setting. I also felt the same insolent, distrustful vibes Kaylen reported. I heard the condescension in their tone when they called to report interactions with Kaylen. It was an "us and them" mentality for the therapists and counselors rather than a team sport. I saw that the intensive outpatient treatment model was not a good fit for Kaylen.

There is no linear, or one size fits all approach to addiction, especially when there are co-existing diagnoses in the physical and mental health of an addict. Couple that with the fact that Kaylen and I were raised to question everything, her participation in a protocol-driven model to deliver services did not bode well. Questioning the medical community's rubric-driven environment was interpreted as not buying into recovery; being deviant and disrespectful. The expectation was to step in line within the hospital's rehab model, and when that didn't happen, the addict was labeled as defiant or manipulative.

Three days shy of completing intensive outpatient rehab, Kaylen quit the program. It felt like a huge set back when Kaylen quit rehab. A part of me ached for her just to step in line and submit to the treatment model; she might learn something. Her spirit could not do it though. She knew it wasn't right for her and there was nothing I could do about it. She was an adult and could do what she wanted. She felt disrespected. I questioned whether I was being snookered. I reminded Kaylen that dad's financial support was contingent upon her being in treatment with regular UAs. Kaylen told me she'd figure it out. I hoped and prayed that she would.

To her credit, Kaylen tried, albeit her way. She focused her efforts on getting back on her own financial feet that required her to fill out forms and applications to get a job. Kaylen stayed with Julee for several weeks until Julee found drug paraphernalia in her house. Julee called to say she could not have Kaylen at her house with what she found, as she had a child in the house. I completely understood and picked up Kaylen's stuff from Julee's house and moved Kaylen's stuff to a mid-town motel located near my office.

When I met with the motel manager, I told him that I was my sister's financial conservator while she got into treatment for addiction. I supplied the manager with a copy of the power of attorney and release of information along with my business card and wrote my direct line on it. I paid cash in advance by the week. Kaylen was settled in a pay by the week place near my office with Uber cards for transportation to find another treatment program.

Within two weeks, the motel manager called to inform me that Kaylen's behavior was not in keeping with house rules. The motel staff reported late night comings and goings and that they could not have Kaylen's manic rage at motel staff in the common areas and in front of other guests.

Kaylen's unstable housing had become a hamster wheel of ongoing crisis. When the motels called to kick Kaylen out, I texted her to pack up her stuff and showed up the next day to stuff her bags of clothes in the back of my car and move her to the next motel. One motel manager provided still shots and video footage of Kyle sneaking in through a side door, and another supplied Ziploc bags of used needles that housekeeping found in her room. Kaylen was kicked out of four motels in one summer.

Kyle was eventually arrested for assault, criminal trespass, and mischief. This was the intervention needed to interrupt the dysfunctional toxic pattern of their relationship. Kyle's drug-fueled antics landed him in jail, which resulted in a forced separation from Kaylen. *No longer would Kyle be a distraction to Kaylen's recovery*, I thought. I hoped Kaylen regarded Kyle's downward spiral into the criminal justice system as something that she did not want to be a part of and that it would induce her to separate from him.

At the next weekly parental meeting, dad rightly asked about UAs. Kaylen hadn't supplied a clean UA since she quit rehab at the hospital, and that was a term of the subsidy agreement. Dad recognized the missed UAs as a weak spot in Kaylen's loosely held, unsupervised treatment plan and wanted to use Kyle's imprisonment as leverage for Kaylen's treatment and to legally separate from Kyle, become independent, get a job and get accepted as a patient at a medically supervised treatment program.

I realized that I was too close; running in the trenches alongside Kaylen, so focused on safe housing that I was unable to see that Kaylen had not supplied a UA. I was distracted from that term of the subsidy agreement, caught up and overwhelmed with securing safe housing for Kaylen within the budget. The perpetual crisis conundrum of her expulsions from the housing accommodations I secured for her was created by her frenzied and turbulent behavior.

Each time I met with Kaylen, I asked her about her relationship with Kyle and brought divorce papers for her to sign in the event his behavior reached a breaking point for her. Each time Kaylen teared up with emotion and steadfast connection to Kyle. Despite Kyle's behaviors, Kaylen remained loyal and devoted to him. It did not feel right for me to push the notion of a divorce on her, as that was a decision only she could make.

Being the family point person for Kaylen was hard, heavy, and exhausting. I delivered the information about Kaylen that mom craved and supplied data to dad to assess the effectiveness of resources and efforts invested in supporting Kaylen towards treatment. I was a barrier to Kaylen's rage and beguilement to mom and field sergeant to dad with reports of her physical health, medical status, and treatment, progress on housing and efforts at employment. For another layer of objectivity, I'd check in with my board of directors that included my therapist, husband, adult son, and posse of girlfriends.

I was emotionally wrapped around the axle at the level of Kaylen and Kyle's destitution and vagrancy. It felt that addiction and I were on a fast swirling merry go round, each holding onto my sister tightly; not letting go, with only addiction laughing and thinking this was happy fun play time. My therapist held private space for me to dump and leave all the heavy weight of destruction and dysfunction in his office. My husband silently supported me with me tea, long nature walks, and prepared meals as I despondently navigated as the ever-changing and unpredictable storm front addiction whirled. My girlfriends sat in disbelief as I relayed accounts of Kaylen's seeming progress that was mitigated by repeated patterns of compulsion and destruction with Kyle.

One day I commiserated with my teen-aged son about Kaylen's latest encounter with the police. He irritably expressed what he had kept from me and bottled up for months, "Mom, why do you give her so much? She's doing nothing to help. You know that she's going to die from this don't you?"

I tearfully replied, "Son, she's my sister. I can't stop loving her. People are in our lives by birth or choice, a reason, season, or a lifetime. Your auntie is in my life by birth and for a lifetime. I know you and your sister would do the same for each other."

Dad grew weary at our weekly dinner meet ups. Addiction was prolific; everywhere we looked there was another story about a life affected by addiction. Addicts were on the street, stories were on the news, in the paper, neighbors and friends were losing loved ones to overdoses. At one of our dinner meetings, dad brought a magazine article about the generational shift of boomers having to care for their children and grandchildren due to their children's addiction. It was an awkward, heavy guilt to feel grateful that Kaylen did not have children and all we had to care for was her and her animals.

In effort to be constructive, maintain connection and a forward-moving pace, I framed weekly dinner discussions with my parents in the positive. I informed them of the progress Kaylen had made in addiction treatment with medication management, that we attended an **NA** meeting together and spoke regularly. At another dinner meeting, dad brought an obituary of his friend's daughter that had died of an overdose. I reminded dad that, "you're the only father Kaylen has, and it doesn't matter if she dies of cancer or addiction; we do not give up on those we love."

It was difficult to speak with Kaylen in person. So, I took to writing Kaylen letters as an objective way to communicate the two steps forward three steps back disjunctive headway she made with treatment, UAs, housing, and employment the past several weeks. Sometimes Kaylen was engaging, other times she was mean. My heart wanted to reach out and hug her; I was so grateful she was alive and communicating with me. On the other hand, I felt she withheld her truth from me. I did not believe her words as her actions spoke louder. The letters I wrote to Kaylen are included in the appendix.

By late summer/early fall, Kaylen found a place to stay for the long-term; at least through the winter, we hoped. She introduced me to the landlord and they both signed a rental contract. She was in a medication treatment program for severe substance abuse under physician supervision. I gave her my mountain bike to get to appointments. I attempted to connect with Kaylen in person at least once a week to assess her wellbeing and progress on other aspects of life. I started to attend support group meetings of my own.

There is no road map for getting out of the forest of addiction and there's no golden ticket when the addict you love qualifies for rehab or a bed opens, or the addict is finally willing to go to a meeting. All of these are big steps in the right direction and deserve honor for the work, truth and love it took to get there. These prayed-for feats that feel like marathon milestones are steppingstones to the start of the real story.

16

The Road to Recovery
by Way of Trap House

SO, WHAT PROMPTS A MIDDLE-AGED HOCKEY MOM lawyer lady to walk into a **trap house**? (*Warning: the occasions I went to drug infested hives to reclaim my sister were brazen, reactionary, and not completely thought out. Drug houses host uncontemplated dangers that traumatize the human senses and possess disturbing sights of vacant people, used needles, powerless sounds, and dank smells. Do not interpret the fact that I write about these expeditions as an endorsement to do what I did. I do not recommend going to these locations. Horrible people and events mix in these spaces including drug dealers, users, and other unstable hanger-oners that cling to addicts like the drugs that grip its' users.*)

It was early October and Kaylen was in the process of moving into the place she had rented. The medical provider she initially saw three months prior agreed to take her on as a patient to treat her addiction with supervised medication management. Her UAs were negative, except for THC. Since Kaylen was not in an intensive outpatient program, dad thought it was important that Kaylen get a job. He believed employment would improve Kaylen's confidence and independence. Kaylen followed up on dad's suggestion and researched employment opportunities. She filled out job applications and went on interviews.

Mom and I travelled out of town to visit my daughter for grandparents' weekend. As I unpacked my suitcase at the hotel, an unidentified number appeared on my phone. I answered with hesitation and wondered if something happened to Kaylen. My anxiety increased when I heard a static pre-recorded message that the call was from the

Anchorage jail. It was Kyle. He asked that I supply him the same assistance I gave Kaylen when she was in jail.

Really? I thought to myself. *You have the absolute fucking gall to ask me for help when it was you and your brother that put my sister in jail!* To maintain rapport, I held my fuming tongue and listened to what Kyle said. I did not want to burn bridges with Kyle since he was still married to Kaylen, and for some reason, probably drug related, Kaylen remained dedicated to him while she battled towards **recovery**. Kyle and Kaylen were still connected in the eyes of the law, but with all the betrayal and infidelity water under the bridge, they were seemingly separated for all other intents and purposes. I told Kyle the truth; I was out of town and not available to help him. With that, Kyle said, "Okay," and hung up the phone.

The next morning, I woke up to my phone blown up with notifications from friends, colleagues, and public safety reports that Kyle escaped from a half-way house and was on the run. Local news media outlets posted Kyle's face on television and the internet and asked the public to help to locate Kyle. I immediately called and texted Kaylen repeatedly, like every hour. No answer. No response.

I did not leave Kaylen messages about Kyle, as I did not want to instigate her into savior chase mode for her man. I had not heard anything from Kaylen during the mayhem that involved Kyle. I was scared that Kaylen was connected to or with Kyle in this latest fiasco someway or somehow. I feared that Kyle would run to Kaylen and that Kaylen's jacked up, reckless mind fucked devotion to him would induce her to run off with him and do crazy shit together, Bonnie and Clyde style, just as they had done several years earlier in Texas and Alaska.

It was déjà vu all over again. Just when I felt a semblance of light, stability, and hope, our family's world flipped upside down and was turned on its head. I was out of town, away from all the bedlam, and there was nothing I could do. I could not drive to check on my sister. There was no one to call. I sent dad and Chris screen shots of the internet postings that Kyle was on the lam. Dad responded that I should get in touch with Kaylen to inform her to stay away from Kyle.

Duh, I thought to myself. *What do you think I've been trying to do? Don't you think I already tried to connect with her? Don't you know that telling her what to do is completely ineffective? That has never worked. Why keep doing the same thing over and over expecting a different result? Even if I did get ahold of Kaylen, I sure as hell would not tell her what to do. I'd talk with her about what was happening with hope that she would arrive at the conclusion herself to stay as far away from Kyle so that she would not be an accomplice to anything.*

Why dad maintained the unreasonable expectation that I somehow had access to a magic wand that had the power to reverse Kaylen's ingrained impulsivity that may be fuel injected with a toxic love spiral devotion to a marriage in name only was beyond me. In that moment Kyle needed Kaylen, and that emboldened Kaylen's commitment to him as the sad façade of love that it was.

Reports of a suspicious man acting erratically were called in to the police. Kyle was the subject of those calls. News reports stated that Kyle ran from the police to a construction site, got into a truck and fled. Police blocked the truck Kyle drove from the construction site near an elementary school, which required the school to be placed in lockdown mode. Kyle then drove the truck into a marsh, got stuck and ran away on foot. The police arrested Kyle on the escape warrant after being tased. Kyle was charged with felonies as a result of that drug-fueled escapade.

There was no perfect time to disclose Kyle's latest calamity within our community to my daughter and mother. I felt the need to protect my daughter from the news that would travel from her friends back home directly to her. I would rather my daughter heard the disturbing turn of events from me. When a quiet moment of just the two of us presented itself, I informed her of the news reports about her uncle. My daughter rolled her eyes, abruptly turned away and said she didn't care about Kyle. She was so done with Kyle and had been for years. She never forgave him for the brash, foolhardy drunken carelessness he brought to the family by way of her aunt Kaylen.

I also wanted to shield my mother from the anxiety and heartache a mom's mind would travel to with upsetting information that the man her younger daughter married was branded as a dangerous felon. I withheld this latest mishap from my mom for as long as possible, until the end of the trip, to expand time and her enjoyment of being with her granddaughter and all of her healthy young friends. I wanted mom to hold the thought that her younger daughter was rowing in the right direction towards treatment for as long as possible. I knew that once I told mom that Kyle was on the run, mom's mind would dart to Kaylen and that we would lose her again.

While at the airport to board the plane home, I refreshed my phone one last time before I turned it off to check for updates or an incoming text or call from Kaylen. It had been seventy-two hours and I had heard nothing from Kaylen. Just then, like a synchronistic miracle and answer to my internal prayers, Kaylen called. She told me that she had left her phone at my office when she signed the rental papers and didn't have her phone over the weekend. *Thank God! That means Kyle could not get ahold of her and he probably thinks that she will not make herself available to him.* There was no mention of Kyle in our phone conversation. I thanked Kaylen for calling and told her I would see her when I got back.

As I boarded the plane with mom, I shared Kyle's criminal activities with her. Mom's response was the same concern dad and I had, and that was that he got to Kaylen. I told mom that I just got off the phone with Kaylen and there was no mention of Kyle. As we got settled on the plane for departure, I thanked the heavens above that mom and I were out of town when Kyle's craziness occurred.

Upon returning home, Kaylen's doctor called to inform me that he would no longer see Kaylen as a patient if she was late or missed the next scheduled appointment. I said that I would make sure she was at the next appointment on time. I reached out to Kaylen and invited her to a long weekend at a resort hotel for a conference I would be attending. I thought it would be an opportunity for Kaylen and me to talk on the drive to the conference, she could relax at the hotel with a nice shower or bath, eat some good food and walk in nature while I attended conference activities. We could talk about the call from her doctor, and I could assess what she knew about Kyle. Kaylen said that she would like to attend. The following Thursday I drove to the duplex she rented to pick her up. No lights were on, no one answered the door, and she did not respond to my texts or calls. I left for the conference without her.

I departed the conference early to stop by and inform Kaylen of the call from her doctor. I parked across the street from the two-story blue-gray duplex. The garage door was open with three men milling about. An older, slightly built white-haired man worked with power tools and directed the younger men on whatever building project they were focused on. I didn't see Kaylen or the landlord she had introduced me to earlier. I remained in my car and wrote Kaylen a note about the need for her to attend the next doctor appointment that I prepared to stick on the front the door.

I finished the note to Kaylen, entered the open garage and introduced myself to the older man. He said he owned the duplex, that he recently returned to Alaska after business and medical appointments back east. After I politely listened to this old salt tell what he thought were funny lawyer jokes and tales of times he represented himself in legal matters, I asked where my sister Kaylen was. He directed me to his son, the guy my sister introduced me to as her landlord. He skulked around broken-down cars and boats in the front yard with a tool in his hand. He was in a blue mechanic jump suit and wore sunglasses. I knew from Kaylen's social media posts that this man's girlfriend recently had their baby, so I congratulated him on his newborn child and asked if he knew where Kaylen was.

He told me that Kaylen was inside the house and directed me to go see her. I ventured into the dank, dark hovel. It was cold; colder inside than it was outside. I called Kaylen's name. Heard nothing. I went upstairs to the dimly lit second floor. Naked lamp stands with bare light bulbs exposed unfinished plywood floors, stark sheet rocked walls and commercial grade orange-black extension cords that covered the splintered floors like snakes.

As I reached the top of the stairs, Kaylen hopped into my frame of vision. She threw herself into an unlit room at the top of the stairs and fell onto a dingy stained mattress. She had a roll of toilet paper in her left hand and a wad of tissue in her right that she held at the back of her leg to absorb drainage of blood and pus her body excreted. She was hurt, bleeding, and needed medical attention.

Kaylen asked why I was there. I told her that I had matters to discuss with her. The sight of her distressed me so much that I had to read the note I had written in the car fifteen minutes earlier out loud to her like I did the intervention letter six months previously.

"Kaylen, these are things I wanted to tell you; one, dad will be here tomorrow at five o'clock to take you to dinner," I started.

"I'm not going anywhere with dad unless he brings my dog, I'm not going anywhere with him. Do I have to call dad to tell him not to come?" Kaylen hostilely interjected.

"Sure Kaylen, go ahead and give dad a call, I'm sure he'd love to hear from you. That'll be a nice phone call," I said smartly, my voice quivering with tense emotion at the realization that I was at the gates of hell in that moment with my sister and had no idea what demons lurked in the corners of this cesspool snake pit.

I continued, "Two, your doctor called and said that he'd keep you on as a patient if you show up on Monday. Three, I am not authorized to pay next month's rent, which is next week by the way, until there is confirmation that you are in treatment. I recommend that you show up for your appointment on Monday, even if it's just a suboxone appointment, so your rent can be paid."

"Fine," she jeered from the dark recesses of the room only her face exposed to me.

"Last," I said trying to bulldoze my way through the sick discomfort in my head, stomach and skin, "call or text me to discuss my communication with the treatment center. If you'd like me to take you to the hospital for the infection on your leg, I'd be happy to."

"I'll take care of myself," she hissed.

"Kaylen have you relapsed?" I asked.

"No, Sis, I get these all the time because I use IV drugs," she admitted.

"Kaylen, why won't you let me help you and take you to the hospital," I pleaded.

"Because I can take care of it myself, I don't even need to go to the hospital. All they do is cut it open and drain it. That's basically all I need to do. I just need supplies and my friend said he'll go to the store and get me stuff."

"What friend, what stuff?" I asked.

"Gauze, alcohol, stuff to wrap it up with," she stammered.

"Kaylen, I'm more than willing to take you. Is that because of drugs recently?" I asked a different way, prodding for information on her status.

"No, I get them all the time, all over the place. My arms are better and this most recent one is on my leg," she said in a lower soft explanatory tone.

I felt an opening and told Kaylen that I loved her. She quickly returned to a defiant, oppositional tone and shot accusations that the family was disloyal. "I don't feel loyalty to any of you that cut Kyle off from the family. Kyle was dropped from the family."

"Who's disloyal to whom?" I fired back.

"You guys, the whole fucking family! Everyone wants me to cut him off," she shrilled with raised voice.

"Who said that?"

"You did," she barked.

"When did I say that?" verbally volleying to the truth of her warped understanding of love, devotion, and care for another.

"You said that you didn't want me to be with someone that would hurt me," she said recognizing that the words that fell out of her mouth were said with care and love for her, not spite towards Kyle.

"Did I say that I cut him off? You just put those words in my mouth, Kaylen," I clarified to her.

"Whatever, it's the same meaning with different words," she fomented in failed attempt to mischaracterize my truth.

"No, you can't define my relationship with Kyle," I told her.

"There is none that's why," she scorned.

"That's right, he's in fucking jail!"

"That doesn't mean you don't have relationship with someone in jail. You can have a relationship with someone in jail."

"I'm not going to," I resolved to her.

"You're not going to have a relationship with him in jail. You had a relationship with me in jail, but you won't with him because he's not the same," she said, again grasping that the words that left her mouth were my deeds in love and care for her, and not malice towards Kyle.

"Kaylen, I was out of state when he called me," I explained with lowered truthful tone.

"I don't treat Chris that way. I treat Chris like he's my brother," she continued.

"Has Chris been in jail? Does Chris give me drugs? Does Chris let me get assaulted? Is Chris ever not there for me?" I asked in rapid rhetorical question style to prove the obvious point that Kyle was a letdown loser.

"He didn't let me, and I can get my own drugs thank you very much," she snarled to have the last word apprehending that she just made another admission to me.

"Kaylen, you are the only person I care about right now," I softly said to her.

"You don't have to only care about one person," she continued to argue.

"Kaylen, there are other people I care about, and you know who they are. You are top on that list. You can't tell me who to focus on, who to care for or who to love and I won't tell you who to love. I'm not that kind of person. Right now, I'm focused on you, and I would do most anything for you," I said standing above her in pure truth.

"Right now, I need to clean this up and I need to be left alone," as she averted her eyes from me.

"I will respect that," I said with resignation, having said my piece and with one more lap I asked, "Is there anything I can help you with?"

"No," she again refused.

"I love you very much. I'd like to help you with your situation," I pleaded another time.

"I love you, too," she said.

"Please go to the doctor on Monday," I reminded her.

"I will," she confirmed.

"Okay, honey, I love you," I said as I left.

"Love you, too," she said as I exited down the stairs towards the first-floor door.

My venture into the drug world was a harrowing experience. I didn't charge into those places on a unicorn, grab my sister, and ride off to the pleasant hills of rehab, although my naivety allowed me to forthrightly enter these foul spaces not appreciating the danger and how deeply my sister had dropped into this world. Kaylen looked and acted like the devilish dregs that surrounded her. There were many facets to her drug-infused temperament that alternated between rage, manipulation, shame, and fear, each of which spewed a different shade of toxic venom. Despite this, I could see and feel the real her and our bond.

I feared that the strung-out junkies in that house clung to her as the pill-popping princess that she was like a plague of locusts. Junkie **tweekers** are unable to care—for themselves or anyone—and will do anything for a fix. Yes, anything. Imagine it, the worst of it, and that is what an addict will do for a fix. The environment is soul sucking and draining.

To add another layer of dark tar to this horrid environment is the constant presence of drug dealers that swarm the block. They know their customers and capitalize on the addict's weakness for gain, including a family's desperate love. Drug dealers and wanna-be-king-pins see addicted loved ones as a commodity; a means to an end. They know the addict is hooked and will do anything for the next fix.

I have no regret for entering the trapped-out motels and houses; just astonishment that it happened, and we survived. Looking back, I'm astounded that I crossed the thresholds of dank dark drug dens and entered the snake pit recesses that harbored barely alive cells of drug users to find my sister.

In retrospect all that I can say is, and I know it sounds hokey, I was moved by love for my sister, led by faith that our bond was strong enough to overcome, bust through and break free of the exoskeleton and thick web of scar tissue addiction cocooned. I felt an impenetrable bubble of love, hope, and faith when Kaylen and I encountered each other in those places. In hindsight, I am in disbelief that I went to pay by the hour motels and drug **dorm** bunkers for my sister. Below are recommendations I share from my experiences of encountering **TAYL** in trapped out places.

※ Have a buddy with you or tell someone where you are going.

※ Have a blueprint of why you are there at top of your mind. It helps to write bullet points.

※ Prepare for the worst that could happen. Stick with the blueprint and remain flexible. I kept a **Narcan/Naloxone** in the car.

※ Plan for contingencies, if this, then that. If so-and-so is there, I plan to say such-and-such or do this and that. If so-and-so is doing this, then I will do that.

※ Know your boundaries and limits

※ Assess the environment for personal safety.

    ➢ Well lit

    ➢ Note entrance and exit

    ➢ Note location of vehicles, people, and animals and respective demeanor

    ➢ Prepare to record for audio or for pictures and video, especially when uncertain of surroundings.

※ Keep conversations short and to the point. Always speak truth.

※ Genuinely help within your limits. Enter with a mindset of how the situation and this relationship can be improved.

※ It helps to bring materials or supplies for TAYL. Ideas include:

    ➢ Bottled water and nonperishable protein rich foods (protein bars)

    ➢ Alcohol, cotton balls, gauze tape

> ➢ Face wipes, toothbrush, tooth paste.

> ➢ Towels and bedding

> ➢ Phone charger

❋ Do not:

> ➢ Give cash to the addict

> ➢ Give credit card or identification information to those that house TAYL

> ➢ Sign or co-sign rental or housing agreements

17

November Rain

KAYLEN DID THE LEAST AMOUNT OF TREATMENT POSSIBLE to manage her addiction so she could secure the monthly housing stipend our family supplied. The subsidy agreement had morphed into payment for Kaylen's housing, cell phone, and food while Kaylen got suboxone as treatment and supplied clean UAs. I was weary and tired of addiction; and the perpetual crises that came with it; Kaylen's demands for help and reach outs from people within her wake. I texted Kaylen that I would be at the duplex to take her to the Monday medical appointment so that she would not be fired as a patient.

The next morning, I drove the forty-five miles in a snowstorm to take her to the appointment and I parked across the street from the duplex. Corner streetlights softly lit the quiet neighborhood. The morning sun rose as the snow fell and brightened the dark atmosphere that surrounded the hovel Kaylen was in. I walked the snowy path to the worn, uncovered wooden steps up to the brown insulated metal front door. Used hypodermic needles poked through fresh fallen snow and empty propane gas tanks scattered along the stomped foot path and front stoop to the house entrance. The snout of a large pit bull sniffed the crisp snow air through the hole where the doorknob was supposed to be. I said something sweet to the dog and knocked on the knob-less front door. The dog snorted and woofed an "I'm doing my job" type of bark to the duplex's occupants.

The top half of Kaylen's body dopily peered out of the second-floor window. She was pale, make-up smeared on her face, and with major bed head garbled, "Sis, I'm not ready."

"Get ready!" I said. "Throw your hair in a bun and get dressed for this appointment. If you miss or are late for this appointment, you will be fired as a patient from this treatment program."

"Sis, I'm not ready. There's not enough time. I'm not coming," and with that she shut the window.

A mixed consternation of afflictions ran through my mind, body, and spirit. Rejection, dejection, anger, grief, and loss as I stood outside in the cold and looked up at the closed dirty window Kaylen was behind as snow quietly fell on me and cooled the hot anger at her for shutting me out after exerting so much energy to get there. My eyes welled with tears and my heart and spirit sank with despondent thoughts that this was how it may end; hypodermic needles on the ground and a dog's nose snorting through the hole of a door to a duplex where my sister shoots heroin into her body—so close to me and yet so far away. My heart sank to my stomach. Like exiting a sauna, hope evaporated out of me and dissipated into the cool, crisp winter air. It felt like Kaylen shut the door on our relationship when she closed that window and chose addiction. I realized in that moment that I wanted addiction treatment for her more than she wanted it for herself. I began to resent my sister. I am the type of person that does not want resentful relationships in my life. It is not the person I want to be. I realized that my help was not helping. I had to step away. I had to let go. I was addicted to her addiction; too attached to the outcome. I grasped that she had to do this herself.

I turned and trudged through the snow to my car and wrote Kaylen a note.

October 30, 11:17 a.m.

Kaylen—I was here at 10:50 to transport you to an 11:15 appt. that was rescheduled from yesterday. You stuck your head out the window and refused my offer to transport you to the appt. The consequence of your behavior/choice is that you will likely be terminated as a patient, thus there is no addiction treatment for you, no medical UAs and thus I am not authorized to subsidize you or your housing.

-Sissy

With winter gloves on, I jammed the note into the wooden door frame with a used hypodermic needle I found lying on the ground. That way, she and everyone knew that I knew. It was a line in the snow that day for me and first step towards **detachment** from my sister. She stood me up for the last time. I no longer understood her when I called. No longer would I reach out to her.

The next day I left town to spend a week with lifelong girlfriends on the east coast. Between flights at the Minneapolis airport, a call from an unknown number with an Alaska area code appeared on my phone. It was six in the morning at the Minneapolis airport, so it was three in the morning for the caller from Alaska. I answered. It was Kaylen. She had received and read the note I wrote and stuck to the door frame. Kaylen verbally stormed at me, saying that I was too involved and a "controlling little bitch." In our thirty-five-year relationship as sisters, Kaylen had never cursed or used a nasty tone with me. In that early morning airport moment, it felt like addiction grinned its evil teeth at me and was winning. At least I knew Kaylen was alive. She was calling me, and the content of her words were coherent and spot on.

At that empty crossroads airport, I mustered all the tempered loving kindness and calm that I could and told her that she was one hundred percent right. I was done. I was stepping away from her. And with that I pressed the red button to end the call, not knowing if I would ever hear from Kaylen again. In my heart, mind, and spirit I knew I could no longer be that closely connected with her. That was a difficult moment. I had never told anyone, let alone my sister, that I was giving up on them. It's not what I do, and it is not who I am. Yet, I simply could not be connected to her, it hurt too much.

Looking back on this moment, I see it as miraculous and defining. There was a short window of time that my sister could call and connect with me. For there to be peace with my relationship with her, there needed to be space between us. I spent too much time and energy reacting to her acts of self-destruction, that peace and serenity evaporated. I was shaking when I boarded the connecting flight. When I arrived in the east coast city airport, I quickly retrieved my luggage and found the nearest store to buy ingredients for a detox bath. I checked into the hotel and drew myself a bath. Just as I entered the steaming hot Epsom salt bath, my sister called. She was contrite. It was all I could do to muster loving thoughts towards her reaching out to me.

She wanted to talk about the rent stipend. For the first time, I approached the conversation like a business meeting and advised her when I would return to town and the terms of which I would get rent to her provided there was proof of treatment. Kaylen relayed the steps she intended to take to become a patient at a different addiction clinic. The next day Kaylen called and was frightened; she was in another pickle. She said she was in a car with her girlfriend that recently delivered a baby and that the landlord (father of the child her friend had delivered) threatened them both and kicked them out of the duplex. Kaylen called me to problem solve for a safe place for the two of them to stay that night. I listened. Once again, I was away and there was nothing I could do about the crisis. This time however, it felt different for me. Not my problem. Not my circus. Not my monkeys. Kaylen said she would figure it out. I wished her well and said that I would connect with her when I returned home. I hung up the phone with the thought that she was alive and calling me.

18

Happy Hopeless Holidays

WHILE I WAS DEALING WITH MY SISTER'S ADDICTION and letting go, my husband was dealing with letting go of his father in a very real way. With hearts already heavy from the past several months of dealing with Kaylen's addiction, our family huddled together shortly before the holidays in a church to say our final goodbyes. Chris and I looked toward the door to see if Kaylen and Kyle would appear to sit in the pews reserved for family. There is an unspoken rule that family, friends, and loved ones appear at a memorial service; especially when it is a family member. Every human being on the planet respects attendance at a memorial service. The world stops when someone you know and care about dies. Even the animal kingdom comprehends the concept of death. Two weeks before Thanksgiving, my father-in-law died. Kaylen did not show up for the memorial and there was no word from her. The community showed up, but not her. That was when I learned to no longer apologize for Kaylen's behaviors and inactions, and that she was accountable for her own actions and inactions.

My father-in-law's passing was a significant family event, and Kaylen was not present for me, Chris, or her niece and nephew. Chris was hurt that Kaylen did not make an appearance at his father's memorial. Our kids were used to Kaylen not showing up for family events. The lack of relationship Kaylen had with Chris and our children depressed me. This vacancy and gap were her doing, and I could not inflate those relationships into something they were not simply because Kaylen was my sister. I was disheartened that my son and daughter were used to their aunt's unreliability and knew that no solace would be found from her. Our kids were nonplussed by Kaylen's lack of appearance at family moments like this; just miffed that their auntie's lack of presence hurt their parents.

That Thanksgiving, my parents volunteered to host the family meal as my in-laws could not muster the energy through their grief to cook or be thankful when their patriarch had just died. I was relieved that Kaylen and Kyle did not make an appearance at that Thanksgiving. So much shields up energy had been devoted to how, when, and if Kaylen showed up and what kind of embarrassing shit-show would unfold. It was an odd relief to grieve over the Thanksgiving holidays without the focus being on Kaylen and Kyle's latest antics.

At the previous year's family holiday gathering my parents hosted dinners for twenty-plus people. Kyle drank dad's expensive whiskey from a pint glass and got ridiculously drunk. My daughter walked in on Kyle's younger brother doing drugs in her grandparents' bathroom. That experience prompted my dad to ban Kyle's brother from their house. It got weirder and more distant for Kaylen when Kyle's brother was no longer invited or welcomed to our family gatherings. Kaylen and Kyle's excuses that they had to work or were sick became accepted white lies for not attending family gatherings.

Kaylen and Kyle did come to my parents' house for Christmas though. Actually, they were there for Kaylen's birthday. Kaylen's birthday falls close to Christmas, and they typically stayed at my parents' house on Christmas Eve for her birthday and Christmas morning. My sister's overnight presence satiated my mom's obsession to know where Kaylen was and whether she would be on time for family holiday gatherings.

It was our parents' custom to host a birthday dinner on Christmas Eve for Kaylen that evolved into the time our family exchanged gifts. Well into her thirties, Kaylen had lists of what she wanted as birthday and Christmas gifts. Kaylen and Kyle never reciprocated on gift giving, not even to their niece and nephew, not even the gift of time or attention.

The usual attendance at the Christmas Eve gathering was our family of four, Kaylen and Kyle, Julee, her husband, their daughter, mom and dad. My parents liked this gathering, as the family was together, and it transported them to a time when Christmas was a delight and filled with joy. Our family of four dreaded this gathering, as it was the Kaylen show with childish antics, she roped her friend and our kids into. It became an obligation for us to attend this get-together when we would rather be home with each other to not expose our children to Kaylen's selfish, immature, buffoonery.

During one Christmas Eve/birthday gift giving/exchange gathering at my parents' house, Kaylen's eyes were at half-mast, and she looked ready to fall over and nod off on my daughter, who sat next to her for a photo. Kaylen's long, dry, drab brown hair was receded at the temples and her droopy eyelids exposed a wretched job of coloring with blue-gray eyeshadow outside of the lid lines. Her fingers were swollen and wrapped around a bedazzled hot pink cell phone that served as an abstract distraction to her disassociated self from the family she had not seen in months. Her puffy booty and thighs were stuffed into dark, tight-fitting jeans like sausages, and she was layered with long sleeve shirts. Her dark, drawn on eyebrows and bright red festive lipstick mismatched her lack of energy as she tried not to slump onto my daughter seated next to her on the long brown leather couch in our family's sitting room. Another shit-show, this time subdued and limited to eight people, our family of four, my parents, Kaylen and Kyle.

That Christmas, Chris and I felt that Kaylen and Kyle were lost. We didn't know what Christmas gift to get them. I no longer gave Kaylen nice stuff, as they abused or lost whatever was given them. I stopped giving gifts that related to alcohol in any way, even branding on clothes. I focused gifts for them on utilitarian items, healthy food or gift cards to gyms or small business restaurants I wanted to support hoping the money I spent went to something good. That year, Chris and I gave them headlamps so they could find their way in the dark.

Fast forward to the year anniversary of my father-in-law's death. Chris and I were doing our utmost best to support his widowed mother. My parents were out of town trying to live a normal retired life of travelling to the places they had dreamed of during their working days. Chris and I were in a neighboring town a three-hour drive away when I received a call from the state troopers. I could not take these calls anymore and handed the phone to Chris. Chris answered and this is the one side of the conversation I heard.

"Yes, I am their son-in-law and owner of the company."

"No, no one has permission to drive that vehicle."

"They are travelling outside the country right now and I am unable to get ahold of them."

"Well, if they have the car then officers need to go to my in-laws' house."

"My wife and I are on the peninsula right now and can't meet you at the house until Monday morning."

Chris hung up the phone and told me that a male and female couple was arrested driving my parents' SUV. The troopers had called our office phone line, as the vehicle registration for my parents' SUV was tied to our office address and number. My parents' home was burglarized, and the troopers needed to meet with us. Chris and I put the pieces together that with Kyle in jail, he may have been an indirect part of this home invasion of my parents' house and that it was drug related, which we surmised occurred from the initial theft event from last year.

Chris and I drove to my parents' house that Monday. It was a sinking, sick feeling when we walked into their house, and everything was gone; even my dad's snow machine jacket and helmet we had specially embroidered for his retirement. My phone rang and the caller ID showed that it was Kaylen's landlord, and that sent shocks through me of considering that somehow, he was connected to the home invasion. When I picked up it was just a butt dial, however all terrible thoughts went through me. That she was dead. That she was making a desperate call. There was so much darkness and suffering that I had to work hard at conjuring joy and spirituality during the most wonderful time of the year.

I hadn't heard from Kaylen since I had given her the letter of boundaries and refused to respond to her rage requests for help. Kaylen was mean, lashed out in frenzied fury, and was a drain on my energy and resources. Last I knew, she was unable to function and care for herself, unable to be in a safe place for more than 30 days, was unemployable, unable to work, and her relationships with men were unhealthy and without boundaries.

I harbored resentment and felt that she squandered all that was given to her. I was concerned that she had slipped too far down the drain of addiction. I was also at an odd peace that I had done all that I could do and had come to terms with the knowledge that I simply was not strong or smart enough to overcome what possessed her.

Kaylen was alone for Thanksgiving, her birthday, and Christmas that year since Kyle was in jail for absconding with a construction truck. I hoped Kaylen would be done with rehab and well on her way to recovery by the time winter holidays and her birthday rolled around. I delivered a letter to her with rent money and $75 for Ubers. She looked like hell. She was tearful and crawled out from the darkness to tell me she could not keep doing this. I told her she needed to get out of there, as they had not supplied water or heat. I did not tell her about the home invasion of our parents' house, since I did not know what she knew, and I did not know what she meant when she spoke to me. She may have referred to the sleeping arrangements, as they were bad for her back.

Julee maintained contact with Kaylen when I could not. I at least knew that Kaylen was alive, albeit in an abusive squalor. I upheld the belief that it was not too late for Kaylen to get well if she really committed, learned to manage her dependence on drugs to repair relations with family and friends, and re-enter the community.

I had stepped away from Kaylen and looked for ways to fill my bucket since being around my sister energetically depleted me. Even thinking about her triggered a cesspit of drained toxins. I learned about advent and loved on my friends and immediate family.

I thought of Kaylen often. Thoughts of her were present with me in the mornings and carried in a pocket on my heart throughout the day. In the mornings, I prayed that she stopped wasting time, energy, and life resources and that she would avail herself to the help and treatment she needed for addiction, so it did not rule her life. I had stepped away from MWBT while I had chased my sister in the trenches of drug addiction. I reinitiated the quiet practice that calmed me and updated MWBT to the current version.

I returned to the self-care basics and focused on what I could control, and that was limited to me. I structured what came within my sphere, my physical environment, eating and sleeping well, music, food, and people I enjoyed. I walked in nature with my dogs, met friends for meals, and planned trips to have something to look forward to. I gave myself facials and treated myself to massages, manicures, and pedicures. I taught myself new recipes and delivered extras to those in need without expectation, including my sister. Each night I submerged myself in detox baths to close the day and enter peaceful slumber. I reset boundaries.

There is a saying that expectations are pre-meditated resentments, and a wise one once recommended cooking your favorite meal, pie, or cookie for the person that most challenges you. When I stepped away from Kaylen, my faith, confidence, strength, and energy improved. My decision to distance from her and set limits liberated me. Her addiction did not define me. I was at peace caring for myself and my immediate family while she twisted in the wind of addiction's storm front, discovering how low her rock bottom was.

I started to speak differently and said, "this is what I think, this is what I want from you, I love you, but I love me too, this is what I need to do to care for me."

I ignored nonsense and refused to speak about illness or disease without boundaries of, "I don't want to discuss this right now, this is as far as I go, this is my limit, I will not tolerate this, sounds like you have a problem, or I'm sorry you're having this problem."

I clarified my engagement with others and asked, "What do you need or want from me?" rather than assuming that what I thought was the best fix for another's problems was the right one, especially as it applied to my sister. I would then choose if I wanted to engage with the others perceived need.

Each morning I lit a candle and set the timer for ten minutes, that was it. It was best for me to deal with RFF thought loops in the morning so that when the thoughts tugged at me throughout the day, I could say to myself, *I already spoke with you about this today. I have an appointment with you tomorrow, same time, same place.*

I would tuck those inconsolable thoughts of her demise that reappeared throughout the day in a pocket close to my heart with kind words that we would meet at our next appointment.

I treated these RFF meetings like I would the dentist. Not my favorite encounter, but it had to be done. Fear was a dreaded thought loop that I got stuck in. I journaled everything that I was afraid of, which included:

- ❋ A grieving call from mom that Kaylen died having been assaulted and overdosed

- ❋ That I would have to identify Kaylen's body

- ❋ Telling my children that their auntie overdosed

- ❋ Planning Kaylen's funeral

- ❋ Writing my younger sister's obituary

- ❋ Walking in the community carrying the cross that addiction took my sister.

I contemplated Kaylen's desolate, drug dependent existence. I meditated on the fretful thoughts that ran through my head about Kaylen's safety and her dismal life. I went to the scary places of deep sadness over the place and position that she got herself into. I cried, sobbed, and contemplated her wretched existence. I allowed gratitude for the fact that she did not have children. I reflected on worst case scenarios, the most awful being her death. Over several days during MWBT I wrote Kaylen's obituary and her eulogy. It was cathartic and oddly liberating when I came to terms with and accepted the fact that she might die of addiction.

During those ten minutes of MWBT, I allowed my heart, brain, and spirit to go wherever it wanted. I allowed myself to think and feel whatever I wanted with respect to my sister. I also contemplated the best-case scenario that she would be clean, sober, and we would have a sister relationship and be a family again. That seemed so unlikely though.

Family recovery groups call this process detachment or "**loving from afar.**" When I first heard the term detachment, I thought it was a separation, cord cutting and giving up on TAYL. I now know its meaning and customized it to fit what I needed.

That December I wrote Kaylen three letters. I don't know if she ever read the letters. By the first of December I informed her that the only reason I was in her life was to confirm that she was in treatment and to supply rent funds. I had detached with love by that time. I wrote my last letter to her by the middle of December with notation of the progress she made with treatment and her attendance at NA meetings.

The week before Christmas, Kaylen called to ask for help. She had been physically assaulted and had no place to go. I picked her up and delivered her to a safe place. I posted a Notice to Vacate at the trap house for failure to supply essential services.

At the start of the New Year, Kaylen finally decided to divorce Kyle, splitting equally the cost of all the damage and destruction they had done along the way. The holiday season was a mixed bag of happiness and hopelessness. The end of a calendar year and beginning of a new is usually filled with expectations of closure or feats attained with hopes of a compelling future. People remember who shows up to life event moments of graduations, weddings, and memorials and don't forget the crazy shit that happens at family gatherings of birthdays and holidays. In our family there are several birthdays over the twelve days of Christmas, including Kaylen's. Our holidays are quieter now celebrating advent, the twelve days of Christmas between Kaylen and my daughter's birthday, with great gratitude and peace.

19

It's Called Unconditional Love

EARLY THE NEXT SPRING CHRIS AND I LEFT TOWN for a break from the cold and dark of Alaska and life in general. The swirling spheres of uncertainty in life felt somewhat manageable now that I arrived at the conclusion that I could only control myself and what was in my sphere of influence, which was not much. I took long walks on the beach and contemplated this new relationship with life, myself, my family, and my sister. I had space to breathe and be. I stood on a barnacled rock with waves of water that sloshed over my feet. I watched the sand swirl in the salt water and realized I was not in control. All I could do was the best I could do in all the relationships in my life, including my sister. In that moment I felt a shift in my stomach, shoulders, and jaws. I later learned that moment while I was geographically apart from my sister, yet still ethereally connected to her, Kaylen had committed to a life of recovery on her own.

When I returned to Alaska, Kaylen had re-enrolled in an intensive outpatient treatment program. Over the next several months she attended twelve-step recovery meetings, got a sponsor, and went to the gym. Kaylen acquired safe housing on her own with a man she met in rehab. She had a recovery tattoo.

Kaylen and I met once a week for dinner, we called them sister dates. We regrouped and problem solved on how to mend her credit, acquire insurance, and other adult responsibilities that fell away while she was in active addiction. Kaylen's physical appearance, mood, and behavior had improved greatly. Her complexion was clear, the swelling throughout her body had reduced and she was actively engaged in conversation at weekly sister dates about her recovery and the healthy relationships in her life.

Eventually Kaylen got a job and worked her way up to a substance abuse counselor at a women's inpatient facility. She even started a parallel profession as a life coach for women in recovery and acquired certifications to teach yoga.

My parents continued to age and were stepping into life as retired people and figuring out how to exist with mom's progressive brain disease. My partner in all things was unanimously nominated (by me) as the best supporting male in a drama and our children rapidly paced towards being independent young adults. I felt the world slowed down a bit and there was space and time to look around and appreciate the fact that I was still standing. My head was no longer on a swivel after all those wicked seasonal storms that blew through our family.

On one of our sister dates, I noticed that Kaylen was quiet and subdued. I asked her what was wrong. She said nothing.

"Kaylen, I've known you your whole life, you're a terrible liar, what's wrong?"

"Nothing," she maintained.

"Everything okay at work, that lady still stressing you out?" I asked.

"The old shuffle lady, that's all fine and under control."

I placed Kaylen's mail on the table, and we laughed that she received *Better Homes and Garden* magazines and never owned a home or had a garden. I updated her on her nephew, niece, our dad who had hip surgery, and our mom who continued to decline cognitively. I told Kaylen that I needed to leave our sister date early for an evening appointment. She said she had a service commitment at the NA convention that required her to leave early, too.

Fifteen minutes before we agreed to leave each other, Kaylen revealed that Kyle had reached out to her. Actually, his younger brother antagonistically reached out to her to inquire if she had seen Kyle and sent her a screen shot of a court view that identified that he was arrested for burglary. We were both surprised, as we usually received notice of police encounters involving Kyle.

"This must be hard for you, Kaylen, with everything you and Kyle have been through." I said sympathetically. I asked how *she* was doing and acknowledged that it must have been destabilizing and triggering to hear from Kyle and his family.

Kaylen relayed that Kyle was homeless and police found him sleeping in an abandon house. He was arrested for felony burglary. The police observed that Kyle had an observable medical condition and took him to the hospital.

Kyle reached out to Kaylen during our sister date. Kaylen invited him to meet her at the NA conference at the hotel. And so, that night Kyle walked out of the hospital, got a warrant out for his arrest, and went to the NA conference to meet Kaylen.

I walked away from that sister date not knowing what Kaylen would do yet grounded in faith that whatever she did would be good by her.

Kaylen and her boyfriend agreed to allow Kyle to sleep on their couch. Kyle contributed with buying food. I reminded her to care for herself. I harbored anxiety that she would reconcile with Kyle, that she would be triggered, that she would relapse. I am thankful that I could hold space for Kaylen, that she trusted me enough to share what was happening. All I could do was live my life and pray that she was graced with the ability to navigate these waters.

At our next sister date Kaylen shared that she, her boyfriend, and Kyle attended meetings together. Since Kaylen worked as a substance abuse counselor, she paved the way for Kyle to enter inpatient rehab and treatment of his drug addiction. I did not tell my parents any of this information. It was not my place to tell them. There are some things sisters maintain between themselves.

I told Kaylen that her support of Kyle during that time and eventually getting him into rehab and recovery was a miracle that required a courageous heart. She did for him what no one else would, not even his family. She was an angel to him. I told her how proud I was of her. Kaylen replied, "It's called unconditional love. I don't think he's ever had it."

Kyle is now sober and has started a recovery group for men. To his credit, Kyle admitted to doing heroin and meth that crazy October day, acknowledged that he messed up big and regretted that his misconduct affected other people.

Looking back on it all, the mettle of my courage was tested, the essence of my being challenged, and my energy depleted. My life was completely interrupted by the throes of addiction. I needed to heal, regenerate, rejuvenate, and get back in touch with the core of my being. That is a whole other evolution and a transformation. I cannot erase what has happened, nor can I get over it or put it behind me. It is part of my being now, what will I do with it?

I still struggle with how to respond when people ask, "How's your sister?" I'm not fond of the word "clean" as Kaylen was never dirty to me. The term sober does not fit, either, as that seems to apply to alcohol abuse. Addiction is a disease for most and with Kaylen it is a chronic use disorder. My sister will always and forever be dependent upon medication to manage addiction, pain, anxiety, and ADHD. I landed on the fact that Kaylen was sick and has a medical condition of chronic substance use and abuse disorder that stabilized and is in remission. She is in recovery and we both continue to restore our spirits, every day. I am super proud of her.

20

Triggered After Two Years

FOR THE PAST THIRTY-SIX MONTHS I drove through life's storms with the windows up and wipers slapping I had forgotten that driving with the windows and top down to absorb life's beauty, calm, and peace was a thing. I was out of touch and off track with who I was and where I was going. I had gotten lost in the chaos of loving a person with a disease and the map I once had to get home was blown out of my hands during the hurricane storms of active addiction.

The trips I saved, budgeted, and planned for the previous year when I detached with love came to fruition. I was on a ten-day retreat, a mini sabbatical of unconditional self-love with an eye towards releasing traumatic experiences that occurred while my sister was in active addiction. I wanted all the internalized shocks, sufferings, and ordeals to fall out of me onto the water's edge to be washed away and dispersed into the infinity pool of life. It was my hope that I would reemerge onto life's highway, look in the rear-view mirror with perspective on what the heck happened these past couple of years, and reenter a normal life.

I was excited about the upcoming mini-leave and packed days before with the thought that an absence from life's responsibilities at the office would allow a dress rehearsal of a remote presence in all spheres of my outside life that would enable me to go deep into an internal life to heal and just be. It felt good to be excited about something earthly sound, to plan something loving and kind just for me amid a harsh world of contained chaos.

The self-unconditional love retreat started with a group trip of life-long girlfriends. We covertly coordinated a surprise birthday getaway for our beloved friend Sharon. It was my job to ride shot gun with her and co-pilot the four-hour drive to our getaway happy place to a harbor fishing town that would initiate the time-out from life each of us so desperately needed. The long drive would allow us to catch up like girlfriends do.

My husband drove the forty minutes from our house to the office so I could meet up with my friend for the road trip south to the tip of the peninsula. As he drove on the highway listening to tunes we both appreciated, I casually scrolled through social media and came upon a video post by my sister. It was a subdued announcement from a hospital room with IVs and bandages on both her arms notifying her online recovery group that the free yoga class she offered was cancelled.

My heart immediately skipped a beat, my jaw clenched, shoulders seized up and eyes welled at the sight of Kaylen's arms bandaged and stuck with needles. In that moment, the sight of my sister instantaneously transported me through space and time to when my sister was in active addiction. Visions of her entire body puffed up and swollen with open sores on bruised legs with red and purple splotchy arms that oozed yellow puss from red inflamed abscess became center stage in my mind. The words from my sister's mouth on the video were mere background noise as I solely focused on her arms, the bandages and IVs. I exclaimed out loud in the car, "My sister is in the hospital, and she didn't tell me!"

I obsessively played and re-played the video over and over to try and figure out what had happened to Kaylen. I read comments to her social media post for nuggets of information and data about her current status. Her response to "WTH" comments on her post was:

> Just continuing to clean up the wreckage from active addiction. It's just a part of life in recovery . . . I wreaked havoc on my body in addiction and my body is still healing. It'll be okay.

My mind was so singularly focused on figuring out what had happened to her that I failed to absorb the wisdom in her mature, real, thoughtful, and knowing response. I texted Kaylen, "Are you in the hospital?"

My husband arrived at the parking lot of our office and I saw Sharon waiting for me. The sight of her was safe and allowed my eyes to leak welled up tears. Unable to camouflage the surreal swirling time warp feelings within me, Sharon and I locked eyes and two-arm hugged with my head buried in her shoulder. All I could do was show her the video post and squeak out words to the effect that my sister was in the hospital and I did not know why. We went up the stairs to my office for my disassociated mind to check in with my officemates and vacantly look at paperwork before I left for two weeks.

I reacted to the buzz and ding of an incoming text like Pavlov's dog. It was Kaylen, she had responded to my text with the singular word: "Yes."

Lack of communication and one-word texts were hallmarks of my sister's MO when she was in active addiction. I automatically dropped down into rescue mode, shifted into four-wheel drive coping strategies used when my sister was in active addiction, and texted "Can I come see you? Stop by?"

Again, there was no immediate word or response from my sister. I interpreted Kaylen's non-response as isolation, disconnection, and to being secretive; oblivious that her lack of response to me could also be an independent thirty-something adult being private about her medical situation. Discerning truth with a backdrop of substance abuse with someone you love is a hazy labyrinth. You may have heard from some in the rehab community that addicts lie and manipulate, but I have come to learn when you open your eyes, perspectives shift, and you can see the addict you love live their truth. I was still blind at this point in time.

I deposited myself in the passenger seat of Sharon's car, full on triggered with complete lack of self-awareness of my condition. Unable to tolerate the radio silence from my sister, I called her cell phone, no answer. I proactively called the hospital and asked to be connected to my sister's room. With a subdued and curious tone, Kaylen answered the hospital room phone.

An overflow of questions gushed out of me; "How are you, what is going on? What happened? Is there a diagnosis? Can I see you?"

Sharon looked at me like I had three heads. I removed myself from her car (and her wide-eyed stare like I was an overly involved helicopter mom) for privacy. It started to rain. I walked toward the building's eaves and sensed Mother Nature's tears shower on me as a synchronistic knowing of what was occurring on the inside of me. Mother Nature and Spirit paired together as wonder twins to activate and let me know that it was okay to cry on the outside. In that moment it was a meaningful consciousness between me and the universe as I stood under the eaves of my office building, tears running down my face as my sister shared her medical situation with me.

Kaylen characterized the hospitalization as minor, and her DIY treatment efforts were not successful. The condition worsened and became so painful and scary that she brought herself to the emergency room for evaluation. Kaylen sounded scared and was distracted by nurses. Kaylen wanted to leave the hospital for a new employment opportunity in a higher paid position. As we talked, my ears heard her memories of past medical diagnosis when she was in active addiction. Her recollections were starkly different from mine. The good news was that she did not have a fever and surgery was not necessary. She was admitted to the hospital on an emergency basis, told to stay for an undetermined amount of time, and an IV course of antibiotics was initiated.

Kaylen was alone and did not have with her the tools that normally eased panic and anxiety, including her journal, books, earbuds, or computer. Here I was again, worried about her and there was nothing I could do. I was helpless to do anything for her, afraid of relapse, thinking that she would suffer and be triggered, completely ignoring the fact that she was probably in the safest place to heal. She was surrounded by medical support and had a fierce internal drive to overcome this latest bump in the road to recovery. Kaylen and I talked for over an hour covering topics of her new job offer, her boyfriend, our dogs, and how or whether to reveal this emerging situation to our parents. Our mom was alone at the house while our dad was fishing in another coastal town, a two-hour drive away with spotty coverage for cell phone communication. We landed on the idea that she would tell dad so he could reveal the situation to mom. We exchanged I love you's and ended the call.

Sharon continued to drive, eased onto the two-lane highway that hugged the mountains alongside the coast for the remainder of the several hour drive and looked through me to the ocean water. Sharon and I had planned this trip weeks before as a first-step launch towards a self-care sabbatical to recover from years of trauma. And there I sat, retraumatized, full on triggered up all over again and completely exhausted. In hindsight, I see this event as an entry into my own recovery; a mountain hike that required me to bushwhack and break trail for this next life chapter. It was physically and spiritually painful for me to drive out of town and away from my sister not knowing what would come of her hospital admission. I returned Sharon's see through to our soul's gaze and with tears in my eyes said to her, "I don't know how this story will end."

"Perhaps it won't, and that's the story," she lovingly offered. We put on our favorite eighty's music, relaxed into the beautiful drive, and absorbed all the good around us.

Kaylen and I maintained text communication about her medical situation for several days. There was no definitive word on a diagnosis or when she would be discharged. Without a computer or self-care tools, she managed the situation the best she could by toggling between hydrating herself with lemon water, meditation, and makeshift bullet coffee. Still in full-bore triggered rescue-fix-it mode myself, I reached out to her boyfriend to assess whether he could deliver mentally stimulating self-care necessities to her at the hospital. No-go; the hospital was not allowing visitors.

I called the hospital gift shop to explore if it had journals and books that could be delivered to her room. That call went to an outgoing voice mail message of reduced hours of operation. Feeling powerless in supporting Kaylen, Sharon suggested I ask a local bookstore if they would deliver to the hospital. I called and spoke with a salesperson, explained the situation of my sister's isolation at the hospital, and like the angel from *It's a Wonderful Life,* the young lady on the other end of the phone stepped up and offered to deliver reading and journal materials herself. *Blessing.*

Over the next several days I checked in with Kaylen on the daily by text or call, with the thought that my voice and reach outs would be of comfort to her. Her continued nonresponse tore me up inside. Kaylen finally said, "Mom just called me."

I froze and felt her struggle, as it was unlikely my sister had gotten ahold of dad, who probably was out of cell phone range on a boat, to inform him of this latest medical development. Also, there is a non-negotiable rule in our family that we do not lie. That non-negotiable is in capital letters when it comes to our mom. The struggle is real; how does an Irish Catholic raised daughter respond to her mom when asked, "How are you doing" and said daughter is in the hospital?

Kaylen and I spoke with each other about how to navigate this latest development. I took advantage of having Kaylen on the phone and asked a litany of personal questions of her medical condition, employment situation, and, without being asked, offered my opinions on how to navigate these aspects of her life. My sister snapped, "You all have got to stop with the not trusting me!" *Silence.*

"Ok." I said and ended the call with, "I love you."

I was perplexed and baffled. I sat with the phone in my hand and contemplated her words. *What did she mean "you all" and not trusting her?* I didn't understand her words and was confused where they came from. I felt that her sharing and us talking was what people that trust each other do. *I do trust her. How could she not know that after all we have been through?*

Perhaps my overdrive care and concern were oppressive and my maternal take-over rescue mode reaction suffocating. Maybe my helicopter hypervigilance of my sister's adulting after a decade and a half of addiction and couple years of managing her own recovery was patronizing, or possibly she thought that her family concluded that she had relapsed. It didn't really matter. Trying to outthink others' thinking is like a dog compulsively chasing its tail into a never-ending spin. In hindsight, I can now see that I was triggered for my reasons and Kaylen was triggered for her reasons. Here I prayed for a normal adult sister relationship, and I had treated my mid-thirties sister like a child. We had to land on a way to love, support, and be with each other in this new normal of our family's life. Someway, somehow, Kaylen navigated conversations with our mom and dad and broke ground in the relationships in her life independent of me, speaking and living and being in her truth and truths of their relationships.

Relapse looms large, like a dark distant storm cloud on the horizon. Relapse is a facet of recovery that our family did not talk about, in large part, at least for me, out of respect for Kaylen's privacy. We share what we choose to share with each other, mindful of each other's sensitivities. In this process I discovered that I have my own triggers and have become conscious of my physical body, heart rate, and breath. I am aware when my body clenches and shakes, and when my stomach sinks, and evaluate what and why the physical response is happening. Rather than contain or stuff emotions, I am aware of and note red flags of resentment, fear, anxiety, or overwhelm. I care for myself like I would a child or best friend and reflect on what would make me feel better in a time like this. I created signature go-to lists (created and signed by me) of what comforts me and eases my pain, anxiety, and suffering to access whenever and however it fits within my spirituality, mental time, and monetary budget, whether it is five minutes or five dollars.

I've come to know that loving an addict is a long walk in the cold rain, and to be prepared by dressing in layers. Each day I check the weather and dress accordingly, and by that, I mean I learn to love and care for myself with a little more gentle grace, mindful of the traumatic backdrop and special sensitivities that surface and work themselves out from healing and loving an addict as the advertised value-added package deal that it is. Indeed, in writing this book I recognized that I internalized unprocessed experiences that needed to be moved. For a long while I couldn't put my fingers on the keyboard without crying. I avoided writing and the physical space in our house I had created to write these stories. I was swept away by the smallest of distractions and had fallen out of nourishing routines of hydrating myself with lemon ginger water, journaling, meditating and walking in nature.

I fell into unhealthy coping patterns of consuming sugary processed foods, which created low energy and detracted me from exercising my brain and my body. I criticized myself as weak, and felt seeping anger and resentments. That low toxic energy set a shallow foundation that allowed me to overlook, ignore and absorb unrecognized triggers so that I could hurry up and get on with a life after addiction. I was hard on myself and rationalized that I did not have time to care for myself with a detox bubble bath, cup of tea, or nature walk, and that I had spent enough time and money on myself, this addiction thing and in therapy and couldn't afford addiction to take any more of my time or money. Hadn't addiction taken too much already? I needed help moving through the traumatic events and moments witnessed during my sister's active addiction and got caught up in the high expectations of myself that I could do this affordably, alone, and on my own.

One thing I learned is this addiction and family disease thing is a team sport. Now I see, feel, hear, and appreciate triggers for what they are to process and honor them for the legitimate pillars of feeling within me that make me who I am. I finally gave myself a break and permission to put writing this memoir on pause. I did things I thought I no longer needed to do because Kaylen had been in recovery for over two years. I fell in love with myself again and took long walks in nature, hot baths, scheduled massages, got my nails done, baked cookies and meals for others, wrote cards to friends, went on walks with people I love, set up therapy sessions to process dark events I shoved in the back of the closet, and started singing again. I played music and made soups that I liked, went sledding, tried new recipes, set up coffee, tea or lunch dates with friends, cleaned out drawers and closets, and donated to shelters.

Sometimes self-care includes space from the people you love. Guilt-free time with yourself to be and shed the thick, built-up layers of all that rained down on you (and everyone else). Rather than being on auto pilot caring for everyone else and handing them umbrellas, I took care of myself in ways that suited me. It's amazing how the universe opens when you slow down and do what's good for you and makes you happy.

I highly recommend making a list of little and big things that comfort you and make you happy. Keep that signature comfort happy list handy, in a place to access and remind yourself of what to do to improve moments that overwhelm you or are heavy or triggering. I promise, like compounding interest, when you love and take care of yourself, your ability to love and care for others increases exponentially. This is especially true when addiction is threaded within the fabric of a family and the people you love. When you love an addict, you've got to love yourself first so you can love them hard, because addicts are hard to love. It is a weary winding road through the turmoil of active addiction, or any brain disease for that matter. Discouraged bouts of rehab, seemingly sustained recovery, constant fear of relapse, and anxiety about what crisis d'jour is around life's corner drains a beautiful mind, body, and spirit of joyful energy. A low energy environment is exhausting and unsustainable. I invite you to open the secret hidden door that transports you from the chaos and grief that infuses the diseased environment to a place of nourishing comfort for the mind, body, soul, and spirit. It is a superpower skill set to recognize and step into those magical pockets of space and time without guilt, apology, or limits and return to the home and heart of who you are. Ideas for a comfort/happy list:

* Breathe and practice using the five senses. This exercise can be done in less than three minutes and is a powerful grounding and centering tool.

* Meditate. First thing in the morning and gratitude at night before sleep.

* Hydrate.

    ➢ Make your own mini spa water and add lemon, ginger, or whatever fruit or herb you prefer.

    ➢ Teatime. Enjoy every moment of this process. Buy your favorite tea, boil the water, and steep for two whole minutes to make the best cup of tea.

* Walk outside for at least fifteen minutes three times a day. Note observations, beautiful things you see, hear and feel on your walk.

❋ Make a date to connect with someone you love and miss. Listen to what is happening in their life. Do not bring up the disease in your family unless and until asked, and even then, have a prepared response that recognizes the good in your current life situation.

❋ Prepare nourishing meals.

❋ Bake cookies or a pie for someone other than yourself, even better if it is someone that is challenging to you.

❋ Water works. Shower or bath. Like teatime, enjoy every moment of this process. Buy or make a delicious bath bomb, draw the water, smell the salts/oils while the perfect temperature and depth for a water therapy session.

❋ Do something kind for someone else or the community. Each year I send the treatment centers Kaylen attended flowers on her recovery anniversary.

21

The Prodigal Paradox

I FELT ROTTEN AS OUR FAMILY HONORED ANOTHER YEAR
of Kaylen's recovery. Mixed emotions wrestled within me; joy sparred
with anguish while aggravation had a staring contest with gratitude.
Guilt steamed from the contradictory notions that simmered in my
stomach while these contrasting mindsets meandered along the bor-
ders of this magnificent milestone I had prayed for. This internal civil
war was exhausting. On the one hand I am grateful to the universe
for the blessings of strength, resilience, commitment, and loyalty that
contributed to what we overcame, and yet I was uncomfortable that
my other hand held piqued umbrage in this family bear hug that celebrated Kaylen's recovery. To add another mercurial layer of emotional
complexity into the mix, our dad had suffered a stroke and was in a
recovery of his own while our mom's persona continued to swirl down
the drain of dementia.

Not knowing whether our seventy-six-year-old dad would survive
the emergency surgery for a bilateral brain bleed, our family stepped
into crisis strategy mode to consider how to care for mom in her cognitively declining state. Mom's dementia was at the point she could
not care for herself or be alone, which was problematic while our dad
was in the hospital. Mom hadn't driven or managed her own finances
in years and was hermitically sealed to dad for caregiving. We didn't
know how long dad would be in the hospital or what his condition
would be if he survived the stroke and surgery. The plan we landed on
was for Kaylen to be at our parents' house Sunday afternoon and stay

with mom on her days off from work during the first few days of the week. Mom stayed at my house the remaining days of the week that led into the weekend so that I could take mom to church on Sundays, buy groceries, and return her to her home and cat.

The first thing Kaylen did upon arrival at our parents' house was to grab a plastic bag and say in an uncharacteristically directive tone, "I need you to come with me, now."

I followed her purposeful pace around our parents' house to every cupboard, cabinet, and dresser drawer while she deliberately took pill bottles of medication and handed them to me to put in the bag and said, "Take these; I don't want to be tempted."

I stood there wide-eyed, naïve, and dumbfounded, not knowing that our parents had such medication, let alone the location and that it was a trigger for her. Like a child learning gun safety from an elder user, I took a mental note of each location and medication content and responded, "Okay."

Meanwhile, my older, grown-up sister self was filled with proxy pride for my sister. Kaylen next proceeded to set herself up in the space we lived during our childhood to stay nights with our mom.

Staying overnight with our moderate to severely demented mom was not easy. My dad spoke of "difficult nights," and I knew mom was easily overwhelmed and confused and would become restless, disorientated, and wander. I observed her sun-downing behavior of pacing while toggling between anxiety and agitation and experienced firsthand her disrupted sleep pattern when she'd call in the wee morning hours not knowing where she was and dart paranoid accusations to me that dad was mean and played tricks on her. Our family quickly discerned the brave face dad had put on mom's evolving and progressive symptoms.

I texted Kaylen the next morning to check on how she and mom were doing. Kaylen quickly responded that mom woke her at three in the morning and was up every couple of hours asking for dad. Kaylen could not get mom back to bed or sleep. Mom got caught in a thought loop that progressed to anxiety, paranoia, suspicion, delusion, and combativeness to the point she was screaming at Kaylen to get out of the house and kicking doors. Kaylen texted that she had locked herself in the bathroom and that she wasn't not strong enough to do this. It wasn't safe for her or mom. Kaylen was full on triggered by the swirl of rage reminiscent of verbal altercations exchanged in that house decades ago.

I drove to my parents' house to relieve Kaylen and retrieve the powers of attorney my dad had to coordinate a medical appointment for mom with our family doctor. I called the physician's office to inform them that my dad was in the hospital and mom needed an appointment to get a handle on what was occurring and stabilize her mood and sleep. Mom expressed confusion as to why she was going to a doctor's office since she felt fine. I gently reminded her that it was to help with the anxiety over everything that had happened with dad. Initially, mom accepted that response. At the appointment, I showed the doctor the texts between me and my sister. The doctor graciously spoke with mom and observed her demeanor direly dwindle when she harshly asked, "Who's the she?" in a disturbed, distrustful tone. The doctor prescribed medication to calm mom's mood and assist with sleep. *Ironic, huh?*

When dad returned from his weeklong stay at the hospital he was depressed, short tempered, and on high alert to get his affairs in order. He made the crucial mistake of going to the internet to research what had happened to him, the surgery, and his new odds on life. He learned that he had a fifty percent chance of dying and discerned that the only reason he was still on this planet was to hold space for mom. He expressed concern about his ability to care for his wife with both of their increasing needs. I piped up that he had a fifty percent chance of living, that there were other people in this family that he holds space for, and shared with him what occurred with mom, Kaylen and the family while he was in the hospital. He recognized and appreciated the adjustments we had all made to accommodate these new needs.

In the ensuing days and weeks, dad discussed his thoughts of giving Kaylen one of his four-wheel drive vehicles, building her a tiny house next to their home or renovating the house to accommodate her and her boyfriend. My initial reaction was wide-eyed disbelief that turned into anger and hurt. Disbelief that he did not remember all the times Kaylen crashed, abused, misused and did not take care of the cars given to her over the past thirty years and overlooked the facts that she had never bought a car, let alone a house, and therefore had never maintained a vehicle, successfully paid a loan or any bills associated with owning a thing like a vehicle or a house. Anger followed that he would give, owner-finance, and otherwise absorb transportation and housing expenses that most people, including myself, work years and a lifetime to pay off. Not to mention the fact that relapse is real and loomed in the background of our family's life, and I did not look forward to taking on security guard duty of a future trap house with two vulnerable adults inside. I was hurt that the small amount of time I had with my dad driving him to medical appointments was focused on his paying for my sister's transportation and housing. My rational and logical mind understood the quid pro quo between my dad and sister. Kaylen was staying at the house two to three days a week, needed safe transportation and there was mutual benefit for the three of them to be closer. Still, I read, examined, and studied the parables of the lost sheep, coin, and son and the story line of the righteous older son resonated right about now.

So, there I was on the eve of my parents seventy-sixth and seventy-seventh birthdays looking through a clouded, dirty weather-worn window with a bitter, brooding filter and seeing the people I love contemplate their brush with mortality while simultaneously venerating their recovery. My self-righteous thinking was on planes of law and merit rather than gratitude and love. I was self-absorbedly unaware of my sister's constant repentant journey at this stage of her life with our parents, doing the best she was able to make up for time lost while she was in addiction. Our parents were understandably elated that their younger daughter was back in the family fold, living her amends, and they reveled in the energy their daughters brought to the table, house and home at this late stage of their lives. I couldn't do this bitter resentment shit anymore. It's so low energy and I wouldn't! I wouldn't go to those dark places and hang them over our heads. We've overcome so much and come too far for that noxious, stinking thinking.

I made a conscious decision to feel incredibly blessed that dad had survived, and that my sister was alive and thriving. I am delighted that we are in each other's lives. I genuinely enjoy her clean and serene company and treasure our time together. I value and appreciate what she brings to the table, including her frenetic support in caring for our aging parents. She and I have developed a unique chemistry that is infused with colorful collaborations that knit us together, highlighted with bright, bedazzled strands woven into an adulterated blanket of insight that warms the heart.

Someone once told me after I was in a serious car crash that "There must be important work for you to do." That got me thinking that there is a reason we are all still here doing what we do. There is a reason dad survived, a reason Kaylen survived, and reason all this has happened. I now see that the warrior practices in the brave new world of addiction conditioned the wisdom I now hold in this post-panoramic world with gentle understanding, quiet immunity, and faithful knowledge that there is something bigger than the shame, stigma, and fear that is addiction, and that it exists beyond limits of cognitive comprehension and is within each of us that confirms the significant role we play.

So far this edutainment dramedy of life has taught me to mark what I call red flag feelings. Red flag feelings stir things up inside in a thoughtlessly flip, reactionary, or dark way. Red flag feelings are barriers to peace, love, connection, and the truth of who you are. Fear and its' stepsibling worry were primary red flag feelings I wrestled with while Kaylen was in active addiction. I was afraid that Kaylen would die of a drug overdose. That we would be *that* family that lost another to addiction, and that I would be the one to eulogize her.

I made an appointment with fear to list each worry and track it to its panic-stricken little squirrel hole. I had a standing appointment with fear each morning when I woke and every night before bed. I practiced the ritual, set the timer, lit a candle, and wrote all the fears and worries in my mind, in my heart, on the shoulders and the ones churning in my stomach and ethereally through my spirit. When I heard the timer sound, I stopped writing, put down the pen and journal and blew out the candle to release and exhale the red flaggedness within me. Blowing out the candle was a practice to release the fears out of me and into the atmosphere so I could walk through my day in peace.

When fearful thoughts of my sister's safety entered my brain to distract me throughout the day, I told fear that we had an appointment in a couple of hours and would talk about it then. I taught myself to meet red-flag feelings head on, face to face, and get to the nubbins of why that feeling was in my life at that moment in time with this circumstance, or person that presented it. This practice brought strong, resolute peace. Imports of the red flag practice were that I had Narcan in my car in the event I came upon someone overdosing. I wrote and practiced my sister's obituary to speak the words within me loud and proud in the event that she died. Fear flags became a piece of cake for me to capture. I was no longer afraid to stand at the gates of Hell as I had already done so to reclaim my sister. Resentment had presented as red flag feeling and required a new playbook. When I feel the red flag of resentment, I turn to gratitude to count all the blessings that I can.

Here are some tools I used to deal with the RFF of resentment:

The Tale of Two Wolves*

A tribal sage tells the story to children of the consummate conflict within each of us, a battle that goes on inside people of a terrible fight between two wolves. One wolf is evil, filled with anger, envy, sorrow, regret, greed, arrogance, self-pity, guilt, resentment, inferiority, lies, false pride, superiority, and ego. The other wolf is good and filled with joy, peace, love, hope, serenity, humility, kindness, benevolence, empathy, generosity, truth, compassion, and faith.

The children ask the wise one, "Which wolf wins?"

The elder replies, "The one you feed."

---

* The story of the Two Wolves is a legend of unknown origin, sometimes attributed to the Cherokee or Lenape people.

5 To Do's With Red Flag Feelings (RFFs)

* Invite a friend to lunch, coffee, or tea and listen. Do not say anything about yourself.

* Create something for someone else. That can include baking a loved one their favorite cookie or pie. Try a new recipe to challenge yourself.

* Attend a support meeting.

* Go to your resource well. Resources include gratitude, blessings, what's working. Don't have a resource well? Create one!

* Write blessings, miracles and gratitude moments on slips of paper and put them in a jar to read at a later time when a reminder is needed.

Gratitude practices:

* Meditate and contemplate three things in the morning and three things at night.

* Journal at least three things in the morning and three things at night.

* The Rose Rule: Roses have more petals than thorns. For every thorn that is thought or spoken, there must be three petals.

* Meet with your Red Flag Feelings.

Three Steps to Meeting with RFF

SET TIME, PLACE, AND MANNER TO MEET WITH YOUR RED FLAG FEELING

Red Flag Feelings can be taken for a walk, preferably in nature. You can also write a Red Flag Feeling a letter or make a cup of your favorite tea to meet with that Red Flag Feeling to have the difficult conversation.

I like to light a candle for my meetings with RFFs as the blow away release practice is cathartic. Be sure to have a timer, as it's easy to lose track of time when meeting with your RFF. You may not cover all the things with RFF in one meeting, that's where standing appointments with RFFs come in.

PREPARE FOR THE MEETING WITH RFF, LIKE YOU WOULD FOR A LUNCH OR COFFEE DATE OR JOB INTERVIEW

Some tips:

* Select the candle (wax type and color or battery). I prefer the naturalness of fire, smell of wax, and watching the flame dance.

* If writing your RFF as a letter, choose the finest pen and color of ink that suits you and handpick the quality of paper.

* If journaling, pick a notebook that serves, lifts, and empowers you.

* If making tea . . . well, you get it, what serves you. I like lavender chamomile.

* Research what you are meeting with, where it comes from, what fuels it, what it likes and why.

INVITE THE FEELING IN LIKE PAUL SIMON WOULD TO AN OLD FRIEND TO TALK ABOUT WHY YOU INVITED IT HERE

* Journal all the feelings, worries, fears, concerns, points, and arguments.

* Contemplate each and track it down to its true source.

* Meditate on where you have arrived. Perhaps an action item has surfaced, or realization that an apology is in order or a living amends.

4 Tips on How to Cultivate Faith, Forgiveness, and Peace

* Look for love and beauty

* Practice acceptance

* Release resentments, fear judgment

* What's my role?

Journal prompts that help move an RFF along

* What Is Your Red Flag Feeling? (Grief, Loss, Fear, Anger, Resentment, Frustration)

* What are ways to curate faith and forgiveness in your life?

A Poem on the Art of an Apology
BY: MKC

How did I hurt another?

Was it words, action, omission, or manner?

No excuses or defenses as that's continued pride.

It's about the other, set ego aside.

Understand the offense and do not minimize

Extol heartfelt regret to apologize.

Afterword

How the Saints March In

AMIDST A FOG OF POSTPARTUM DEPRESSION, I stood in the lobby and smiled at guests outfitted in attire for the baptism of our first born. Family trickled into the pews of the church; the same church I had gotten married in a year and a half earlier. It was a mid-summer Sunday morning. My husband Christopher paced about the foyer muttering lines of a poem he specially selected to deliver at this auspicious religious event. My mother-in-law proudly held her only grandchild. I was thirty-years-old. Kaylen was sixteen. I specially selected her as the godmother for my first-born son, her nephew.

Kaylen wore a white, short sleeved shift dress with a white single button cardigan clasped at the base of the notch on her neck. She shifted her svelte, athletic body from leg to leg in age-appropriate half inch white ankle strap heels as friends and neighbors from the community passed through the entrance. With anxious anticipation of the sacramental role, my sister and thirty-something-year old brother-in-law moved from greeting guests at the front of the vestibule to the back corner of the church.

The deacon shuffled toward the four of us baptism participants like a poppa penguin herding chicks, his arms circling in outstretched fashion to usher us deeper into the back corner. With a hushed, down low voice that contained his wide-eyed tizzy, the deacon whispered to our team huddle, "This child can't be baptized."

Like team players that don't understand coach's direction, we snapped our upper bodies back and exchanged puzzled looks.

156

"What does that mean, exactly?" I asked.

"Your son's first name is a surname, his middle name is also a family surname, and the last name, well, it's a surname too. None of these names are a saint's name. A saint's name is needed to baptize this child," the deacon responded.

"What the heck? The church is full of family and friends for this baptism. This has been planned for weeks and we're just learning of this saint's name thing now," my rarely church going husband piped in.

He exited the huddle and continued to pace and murmur to himself.

"What can we do?" I asked.

"You can give your son a saint's name for baptism purposes," the deacon said.

Like a low orbit satellite, Chris made another lapped revolution around the baptism participant group and with a muttered bluster snorted, "All these church rules. A saint's name? I don't know any saint's name!"

Chris turned to Kaylen and with a wise, curious crack asked, "Who's that little boy character in *Where the Wild Things Are*? What's his name?" An attempt to tap into their shared appreciation of children's literature.

Kaylen laughed out loud. "You mean Max, like Mad Max?" Her teenage smirk validated Chris's newbie attempt at being a religious rebel.

"Yeah . . . Mad Max. Is there a St. Max?" My husband asked the deacon.

The deacon looked in the saint book and said, "Yes! There is a Saint Maximillian!" And with that our son, my sister's nephew and godson, was baptized in St. Maximillian's name.

Fast forward a decade and a half. I'm at a yoga retreat in Palmer, Alaska, with two lifelong girlfriends, the weekend before the intervention with Kaylen. The three of us had not seen or been with each other for a while. We are part of a solid soul sister group that have been bestie chums since elementary and middle school, through multiple decades of life events that include first kisses, high school, college and grad school graduations, boyfriends, marriages, births, divorces, family illnesses, and deaths. We have been in each other's weddings, to the births of each other's children, and our kids call us Aunties. We are the type of pals that when we're together, we are instantaneously transported to our young, non-judgmental, unknowing, and safe learning slumber party days. Our friendships have evolved into a tailor-made bubble where we hold space for each other that allows uncertainty to be and unfold. We connect on life issues that swirl about and sometimes consume us in the contemporary, uncertain adult times of our lives. Now that we are adults, the times we make space for each other are precious and anyone in the vicinity of us sees it.

One of the girlfriends was in the process of selling her house and asked for tips to expedite the process. The other girlfriend piped up with, "Do what Grandma Kelley said and bury that saint's statue in the yard; your house will sell. I did it and it worked!"

My grandma consistently said there's a patron saint for everything and that praying for their intercession on what is before you can only help. The patron saint of home and family is St. Joseph the carpenter, and there's a Catholic tradition of burying a statue of Joseph in the yard of the home property you are selling for a favorable outcome. As these words and ways of my deceased Irish Catholic grandmother tumbled out of me, my mind popped that there's got to be a patron saint of addiction that I could pray to for intercession. I immediately Googled patron saint of addiction and there it was. It stopped me in my tracks; the patron saint of addiction is St. Maximillian.

Fast forward several months and I am at one of the last affordable motels that would take my sister. I developed a routine to build rapport with motel front desk people and managers when I rented rooms for my sister. I paid a week in advance, supplied copies of the power of attorney my sister granted me with my business card so they could contact me. This latest space fit Kaylen's housing needs with a single room, bed, and a separate communal kitchen that had a fridge and laundry. The motel was located on my commute out of town that would enable me to stop by after work. Unfortunately, the only room available was on the ground floor. I expressed to the front desk manager that a ground floor room was not safe for a single woman. The manager confidently verified that safety is a priority and showed a row of television monitors of various camera angles that were regularly watched of the motels exits and access points, including the ground floor rooms. With that assurance, I paid for my sister to stay there for a week.

In less than two days the front desk manager called and said Kaylen could no longer stay there as she had broken the house rules. He requested that I come by to collect her belongings and said that he would refund me the rest of the week that I had advance paid. When I arrived at the motel, the front desk manager apologetically showed me video footage of the ground floor window to the room rented to my sister. I recognized the man accessing my sister's room through the window as her husband. There was also footage of him and another man entering the motel after curfew by a side door that was propped open. The front desk manager also pulled out a baggie of needles the cleaning staff had found in my sister's room. The front desk manager remarked that he could tell my sister was actively using the moment she walked in with me saying, "Wearing sunglasses at night to cover the eyes is a dead giveaway."

That thought never occurred to my sister-loving mind, as I thought the sunglasses were stylish and looked good on her. Nevertheless, I appreciated his honesty and the personal effort for my sister's safety, none of which he had signed up for. We exchanged what pleasantries we could under the circumstances, with the unspoken knowing of the uncertain road I was journeying with my sister, and he asked, "Anything else I can do for you?"

> Me: "Well, if you're a prayerful person, please pray for my family. This has been really hard for us."
>
> Front desk manager: "Okay, I don't normally pray but I will for you. What prayer should I do?"
>
> Me: "Well, I'm Catholic and there's a prayer to a saint for those that are addicted. You can pray that prayer or to that saint."
>
> Front desk manager: "There's a what; a who?"
>
> Out of the corner of the motel lobby a man slouched on the couch perked up and said, "Yes! There's a patron saint for everything!"

Me: "Yep, he's right! Do you know the patron saint of lost things?"

Motel guest: "St. Anthony! Dear St. Anthony please come round, something's lost that can't be found! Works every time!"

Me: "Do you know the patron saint of animals?"

Motel guest: "St. Francis. Pray to him when your animals are sick. Right now, our family is praying to St. Peregrine."

Me: "Patron saint of cancer. I will pray to him for your family as well, sir. Do you know the patron saint of addiction?"

Motel guest and front desk manager both responded, "No, there's a saint special for addicts? Who is it?"

Me: "St. Maximillian."

The front desk manager's mouth dropped, and his face became off color, like he'd been visited by a spirit. Seeing this change in demeanor, I asked, "What's wrong?"

He pulled his jacket aside to reveal a name tag that said "Max".

Prayer for Addicts to St. Maximilian Kolbe, Patron Saint of the Addicted

St. Maximilian Kolbe, patron saint of the addicted, I come before you seeking your assistance and prayers for all those suffering with addictions, especially (name person[s]).

Pray that God will help (name person[s]) break the chains of addiction that hold him/her bound and set (name person[s]) free to live a life of health, happiness, and hope.

Ask the Lord to look with compassion upon (name person[s]) and in His infinite mercy to fill his/her life with people who will hold him/her accountable for his/her actions and help him/her stay away from that which held him/her bound.

If (name person[s]) must seek help to overcome his/her addiction, pray the Lord will lead him/her to the best help available.

I ask all this in Jesus's Name. Amen.

Serenity Prayer

God grant me the serenity
to accept the things I cannot change,
the courage to change the things I can
and the wisdom to know the difference.

Ho'oponopono Mantra, Prayer and Mediation

Hawaiian practice of reconciliation:
I'm sorry.
Please forgive me.
I love you.
Thank you.

Prayer of St. Francis

Lord, make me an instrument of your peace:
where there is hatred, let me sow love;
where there is injury, pardon;
where there is doubt, faith;
where there is despair, hope;
where there is darkness, light;
where there is sadness, joy.
O divine Master, grant that I may not so much seek
to be consoled as to console,
to be understood as to understand,
to be loved as to love.
For it is in giving that we receive,
it is in pardoning that we are pardoned,
and it is in dying that we are born to eternal life.
Amen.

Prayer to St. Michael

Saint Michael the Archangel, defend us in battle. Be our protection
against the wickedness and snares of the devil;
May God rebuke him, we humbly pray;
And do thou, O Prince of the Heavenly Host, by the power of God,
thrust into hell Satan and all evil spirits who wander through the
world for the ruin of souls.
Amen.

Epilogue

By Leonard Thom Kelley

WE COULD NOT IGNORE OUR DAUGHTER'S self-destructive behavior that could have resulted in losing her life. As a family, we rejected a "tough love" approach and chose rather to be proactive to positively encourage Kaylen to enter treatment. We were willing to take the risk of caring for someone we love and investing the emotional and financial resources Kaylen required.

The initial attempt at intervention was expensive and did not work, but was useful to show Kaylen that family and friends were concerned about her even if she was not yet ready to enter treatment. No case is hopeless. Family love and engagement can be a powerful source of positivism for an addict.

This is not the end of Kaylen's rehab and recovery. Kaylen has developed a recovery program that fits her. She has discovered a purpose and mission to counsel and stand with others dealing with life skill difficulties in addiction and recovery. Kaylen has over three years of sobriety, a job and loving relationships with family and friends. We are thankful.

Sadly, I have witnessed several friends grieve the loss of their children to addiction. They, too, invested in their children's treatment. The death of a child is something no parent and family ever recover from. My wife and I will forever walk with families that have lost a loved one to addiction.

As I write this, I am in a rehab and recovery of my own. I suffered a stroke, with bleeds on both hemispheres of the brain and underwent a bilateral craniotomy. My health is such that I can no longer care for my wife, who has dementia. I am blessed with the same proactive and positive support from my daughters that was devoted to Kaylen. It is a parent's true blessing when life comes full circle with your children and family adjusts their lives to provide support to their parents.

Appendix

Intervention Letters

Dear Kaylen:

I am writing this letter because I love you and I want to help you end your addiction to drugs.

I remember the effort and energy you exhibited after you broke your ankle at the Whitehorse Artic Winter Games. Mom and I flew you back to Anchorage and the doctors successfully operated. Your recovery went well, and you played college soccer because you rehabilitated your ankle successfully.

I remember a girl who enjoyed having friends over to the house and enjoyed life. A girl who did well in college and earned both BA and Master's degrees. You were on the road to be a great therapist because you are a caring person; the person I love.

Over the last several years you have changed. You stopped hanging with your friends and family. You would come late to family events—if you came at all. If you did come, you were generally impaired by drugs.

Your addiction has become so noticeable that I cannot interact with you—not because I do not want to but because I cannot deal with seeing you being ravaged by drugs.

You are a sweet caring person by nature—but drugs make you mean spirited and not nice. Your addiction is noticeable and serious—but you can beat it IF YOU TRY.

Mom and I want you back. We will help but you must act, by receiving treatment NOW.

Love, Dad

Dear Kaylen,

I am writing this letter to you because I believe that drug addiction/
consumption continuously negatively interrupts and damages your
life. As your mom, I love and care for you and I hold in my heart many
proud memories of your accomplishments and achievements—not to
mention your courage and compassion for others. When I am in my
home office, I cannot help gazing upon the many pictures of you on
my wall—each picture captures your essence as a beautiful daughter,
loving aunt, delightful niece, wonderful sister, outstanding athlete and
good student.

I have always been amazed at your zest for life---I could not possibly
count the number of soccer games your father and I attended. Often-
times you were one of the smaller players—but that never got in your
way! You consistently charged forward and seemed to fly down the
field at the amazement and disappointment of the other team. During
high school your energy level was remarkable—go to school, followed
by soccer practice, speed skating, pageant practice on the weekends
and of course the Arctic Winter Games, in which you performed well.

After you graduated from high school and attended college and
graduate school, I was so proud of you! You maintained good grades in
undergraduate school while playing soccer. I was delighted when you
were accepted into graduate school for a Master's in counseling. Once
more you consistently maintained good grades while in school full
time and working part-time. You performed well in graduate school
and in the placement agency. Your counseling skills were excellent.

While your drug addiction is serious, it is not insurmountable and
can be dealt with. Your family and friends believe that your going into
treatment is important. **We all miss the Kaylen we knew so well.**
We all believe in you and your ability to overcome the addiction that
haunts you. I miss the fun, the activities and successes. It is time to for
Kaylen to return to the family and friends that love her. To get there
it is important that you receive treatment. Your future can become
bright once more. **I WANT MY WONDERFUL DAUGHTER
BACK!** I miss the fun we used to have and role you have played in

this family. Remember, when **you dad** and I were babysitting Connor (about three weeks old) and he **would** only stop crying when you held him. When you gave him to **me or dad** to hold—he would immediately start crying!!!

Your going into treatment is **important**—you deserve to recapture your bright future filled with success. Your family wants you back—we miss you—I MISS YOU!!!! I **ask you** from the bottom of my heart to accept the help that is being **offered** to you today. I hope and pray that you will accept this opportunity.

You are an important **member** of our family—we love you and want you to be healthy and **happy**. Your entire family hopes you select treatment for a happy future. **Until** you go to treatment you will need to secure a place to live, and I **will no** longer provide you with money. However, what I would really **like** is that you accept this opportunity to go to treatment and get the **tools** to live your life joyfully and successfully on life's terms. I hope **you will** accept the gift we are offering you. It is a chance to get the **help** you need to stay clean and sober. You deserve to live a happy, **healthy** and productive life. I hope and pray you receive the professional **help** with detoxification from drugs.

Kaylen, you are my daughter **and** I want you to recapture your life—the life you deserve! I **hope and** pray you to go into treatment TODAY—as does the rest of **your** family. We all want to see you happy, healthy and untangled from the nightmare and destruction of drug addiction.

I love you Kaylen as does your whole family; please accept the help that is being offered.

P.S. If you elect not to accept **this** offer of help, it means that I will no longer be available to help **you;** to listen to you when you call me in a crisis, when you tell me **you** are a victim or that you are in jail.

Dear Kaylen,

I remember being the flower girl at your wedding. I remember playing soccer with you when I was little. I remember going to the movies with you and Connor . . . I love these memories so very much because they all bring happy thoughts and are all with you. The moments we've had together I cherish and would never want them to end.

When I heard the news about the addiction, I got scared because I thought I wouldn't be able to see you again. But then I realized that this could be a chance; a chance to make all the memories we used to and to be able to spend time with my aunt. I want to see you succeed and I want to see you smile. I loved seeing you smile when I used to get my white-hot cocoas at the café you worked or when you made Connor and I wear those really big and fluffy bear costumes. I never want to see you hurt and I never want to see you unhappy. I hope you take this opportunity and use it to be able to spend those moments with Connor and me.

I will forever be your little flower girl, I will always be your niece, and will always be on your side. I love you so very much, and only want to see you get better. I love you.

Gracie

Dear Kaylen:

I am here because I care about you and want to see you feeling secure and confident in your life. As your brother-in-law, I've known you since you were in high school. You were confident then; not afraid of losing a big sister to a fiancée that might take her away, but welcoming and embracing a new addition to your family. Your quick wit, love of laughter and striking looks made you a charismatic personality that could charm any stranger. You instantly sought a way to connect; seizing upon the fact I was an English lit major in college, you shared that common interest, coyly gifting provocative books with your impish humor. Your passion for sports engaged your fiercely competitive spirit.

I remember attending your high school graduation; "oohing" at your beauty pageant; watching you run the soccer field at college and cheering for you at your first Arctic Winter Games. The bridesmaid at our wedding, you were there to welcome a nephew and later a niece into the family. And when you married Kyle, I was honored that you placed your faith in me to officiate. There have been birthday parties, Easters, Thanksgivings, Christmas Eves. And the kiddos looked up to their athletic Kaylen and loved to have her watch their hockey and soccer games.

But there has been a sad change over the last few years as you've grown further and further away from the family you should keep close. There were too many declined invitations and empty seats at holiday family gatherings. There were too many squandered opportunities to share your enthusiasm for sports with your nephew and niece who both would have loved for you to cheer them on at their games, to share their excitement, and to encourage them to give it their all just as you had done in your youth. There were too many missed appointments where Michaela would come home to me crying at the disappointment of being "stood up" once again. I hated to see that disappointment; watching my wife set herself up again and again for what I dreaded would be another no-show by her sister; setting places at a table that would never be occupied.

That steady withdrawal from family was a strange contrast to the way things started . . . the eagerness you (and later Kyle) had once shown in expanding the family connections. When you came down to Seward last summer to celebrate my 50th birthday, it was a pleasant surprise to see you again at a "family function," and I had a glimmer of hope that the connection would be restored. But that visit was bittersweet, too; marred by the erratic behavior and your late, late arrival having decided to spend time at a different campground beforehand; just like the Christmas Eve party tainted by the drugs Kyle's brother brought to your parents' house and making a spectacle obvious to our children. These days the only appearance you will make with family is to attend your own birthday party on Christmas Eve. This November, after your sister and I spent a week at Providence at the side of my father, who was courageously facing his final breaths, you didn't even bother to acknowledge his passing by attending his funeral right here in Anchorage.

It's to the point now where it's simply pointless to extend the invitations to dinners and set a place at the table; certainly, not fun to have Kyle drinking my single malt scotch from full pint glasses, if you two even appeared anyway. And I hesitate in apprehension as Michaela and I walk down the driveway into the woods for our daily walk with the dogs, because what is supposed to be a refreshing and uplifting experience now becomes another teary-eyed trudge trying to console your sister and wrestle with her angst over your dire situation, ruining the start of the day. I am now reluctant to be near you and Kyle at all, and certainly don't want our kids to be around you because of the scary and dangerous pall hanging over illicit drug users like you and your new crowd, and I don't want any such associations made or connected in any way with my immediate family, or bad influences brought to bear on Connor and Grace.

The company you keep can be a blessing or a curse. And company is something that you can choose. I fear that the company you choose to keep has cursed your ability to live a secure, confident and satisfying life. Time marches on and is relentless in distancing the past from the present. The present is ugly. Continuing down this road of drug addiction arm-in-arm with shady losers will rob you of a past as well as a future, as those distant pleasant memories with family and true friends will become erased by the present ugly events and replaced by a grim and isolated future. Please take courage now and turn your cheek from that sad darkness toward the light that a change of circumstance will provide. Get yourself away to a treatment facility. Channel your competitive spirit and put it to work to effectuate a turnaround completely that can only be afforded now before it's too late. Take heart in knowing that you can connect again with the family that loves you and revel in shared events that will put a smile on your face again.

Love, Chris

P.S.—If I have to read this paragraph, then it is unfortunate. You are not perceptive enough to grasp the seriousness of the trouble you are in and not reasoning well enough to appreciate the great opportunity your parents have afforded you to get you quickly to a secure place where you can find your true self again and right the course without the distractions of worrying about how to get your next meal or money to wash your clothes, etc. But a reckoning must be made. You are thirty-five and have to realize and take responsibility for the choices you are making. If you think you can survive alone and make do without a coordinated and professionally guided recovery program and plan, then I disagree and I refuse to be a part of the sinking ship. Please know that the consequence of your refusal to go to treatment will be that my family will not have anything more to do with you until you do. Not only will there be no more family gatherings at our home, but no other communication or contact with me, Michaela, Connor or Grace. There won't be opportunities for you to share in celebrations, camping trips, hockey games, or anything else that the family does; no new photographs to preserve fun moments in time. I simply cannot have us wallowing in sadness, pity, anxiety, or fear of what dangerous and unhealthy conditions you face or may introduce to our family. We just can't allow ourselves to be sucked into that black hole and be hurt and broken, too.

Kaylen, you are my sister, godmother of my son and Auntie to my children. I remember when mom was pregnant with you, and we decided your name would be half mine and half dads. The day you were born, it felt like a blessed gift on that Christmas Eve—a child that mom, dad and I hoped for as mom had been told she could not have any more children. I changed your diapers, watched you after school while mom and dad worked, picked you up from daycare and school, nursed you when you had broken hearts and a broken ankle. At the age of 14 you were maid of honor in my wedding.

I adore the sweet spot you have in your heart for animals and humans that are misunderstood and struggling. I've admired your natural beauty, athleticism, your nonjudgmental and caring perspective and your love of music. You're the only one that understands and appreciates my adoration of Prince, Bowie and all things 80s. You've been there for me when I don't understand my children's teenage athletic minds, Connor's moods or how Grace is to compete in such physically demanding sport. You've also been there for my husband and children when I couldn't—when Connor issues a hurtful text to his father or an ex-girlfriend's moms chews my son out for breaking up with her daughter.

Your fierce passion for adventure combined with soft creativity, playful sense of humor to take on challenges makes you the rock star I know, love and appreciate. I've always believed in you and care for you deeply. The past several weeks I've cried in the mornings, in the middle of the day and at night, unable to focus knowing you may not be safe, sound or are suffering.

You have not been you, and over the past couple of months it's gotten to the point that I barely recognize/know you. We no longer have sister time/dates. You won't even meet with me—you don't look me in the eye. We don't talk anymore; it has devolved mostly to texts, and even then, you rarely respond. If there is a phone call from you it is a crisis. Your words do not make sense and you snap at me when I try to help, and you doze off during conversations.

You get frustrated that I won't give you money and yell at me. You told me you don't remember the conversation/promise made when dad placed the needles, he found in his bed in front of you at the restaurant. You were nodding off/falling asleep during that conversation.

We were to meet every Sunday at the coffee shop, that was to be our time—the reminder still comes up on my calendar, but you rarely showed up and if you did it was late.

We made plans to go on a yoga retreat together and you stood me up. I waited for you at the coffee shop for over two hours with a London fog for you and one for me, an extra mat and journal I bought for you. Every night you told me you would come, and you never did. I was really looking forward to that time together just you and me. I'm sad and disappointed that I can't rely on you, or even talk to you about what is going on in each other's lives.

You've stopped attending family functions like the kids' birthdays, Thanksgiving, Christmas, Easter and even the little ones that used to be our favorite like St. Patrick's Day. You have missed out on exciting stuff with the kids that we wanted to share and rejoice in with you.

You do not invite me into your apartment/space, even when I'm dropping off food when you are sick. I have to leave food on the knob/handle. Our relationship has turned to me saving you.

The night you were arrested I was worried sick. The thought of you and Kyle resorting to physical violence makes me sad. It broke my heart to see you at your arraignment and to read your social media pages of infidelity. Seeing you behind the glass in an orange jumpsuit was heartbreaking. You are giving your account numbers away to nonfamily.

I'm afraid when my phone rings and it's a number that I don't know that it's a call about you—another car crash, in jail. Your life has become unmanageable. You're smart, you're funny, you have a lot to offer our family and the community as a counselor and human.

I'm worried about your health with infidelity, disease and use of needles. I want my sister back. I want my kids to have their rock star Auntie back. I want to spend quality time with you, hike with you, walk our dogs together, go on yoga retreats together, make health choices together, have regular lunches and coffee dates. I'd like us to have a real adult sister relationship. I'd like you to be the Auntie Connor and Grace know and love- it means so much to have someone else other than mom and dad to confide in.

There is help for the anxiety that grips you. There is no shame in receiving help for the demons you wrestle with. You can have a safe, supportive space to detox and recover from all the demons. You will have my support if you accept the help that is being offered here today. I'll write you like I used to when I was in college. You are a smart young woman with a lot to offer our community. I want to see you live the dreams we talked about. I'd like to see you happy, balanced and clean. Please accept the help we are offering here today.

P.S. If I am reading this it means that you decided not to accept the help and support we are offering you and chose a path that leads another way and away from our family. I will no longer be available to you to give you guidance or assistance. If you are in another car crash, or have legal troubles—I will not be available to you. I will have to advise Connor and Grace of your choice and our parenting decision is to not invite or associate with you. I will not give you food, money or pay for things.

Addressing Objections:

Homeless
No money
Dog
Cats
Stuff, Moving—deadbolt on door
Professional license

CONSERVATORSHIP OF HOUSING SUBSIDY FOR KAYLEN

This agreement of limited conservatorship addresses and otherwise encompasses family financial resources for housing subsidy of Kaylen. Starting January, Kaylen's housing will be subsidized **provided** clean UAs are supplied. These family financial resources for Kaylen's housing are for Kaylen alone and no one else. If Kaylen chooses to cohabitate and otherwise continue a relationship or association with her husband or any other person, housing subsidy will cease unless Kaylen and proposed co-habitant have a job and are able to pay half of the rent; then family housing subsidy will be at an adjusted rate.

Housing subsidy will not be supplied to support drug use or criminal activity of any kind nor in any way, shape or form. Drug use or criminal activity at housing premises that Kaylen's family subsidizes will be considered an automatic breach of agreement and will result in stay and termination of housing subsidy from family.

It is understood that Kaylen is committed to and currently in recovery for chemical dependency, and in order to receive family housing subsidy will continue to regularly participate in treatment for sustained recovery. It is Kaylen's responsibility to supply clean UAs to her sister, Michaela in order to confirm treatment and receive family housing subsidy.

It is further agreed that Kaylen will continue to take steps to secure employment as soon as possible, in exchange for the family housing subsidy.

It is known that her family loves her very much, honors her strength and commitment on the road to recovery from chemical dependency and to make healthy, independent steps toward sobriety, and all parties to this agreement look forward to receiving continued clean UAs from Kaylen and her sustained recovery.

Dated this _____ day of_____.

_____

Signed: Kaylen and Michaela

Michaela's Letters to Kaylen

September 2018

My dear sister Kaylen,

I write this note to clearly communicate and reset boundaries considering the series of relapses. I also understand that minutes on the phone Julee obtained for you have expired, so we are left with old school letter style communication—or you can call me from room phone that allows outgoing calls.

First, your honesty re: relapse is appreciated and your decisions to increase to bi-weekly UAs and reach out to outpatient treatment clinics is demonstrative of your commitment to recovery. We are discouraged, however, in your inability to keep appointment with the clinics, even when means to attend those appointments are supplied with rides and hundreds of dollars in Uber cards.

Please know that your stay at this motel expires this Wednesday. Your recovery journey to sobriety will continue to be financially subsidized by the family ***provided*** there is participation in a structured treatment recovery program with the therapies we discussed at the dinner with group, individual, family therapies that are augmented with medication management by your physician to supply UAs. It is your responsibility to enroll in a structured treatment/recovery program that provides the therapies you want, to be on time to appointments, attend treatment and supply UAs for continued housing to be subsidized by the family.

Chris and I plan to stop by **this Saturday (tomorrow)** to drop off the bike you and I texted about. It would be good for you to arrange to show us the place you found and coordinate move-in this Wednesday, as winter is swiftly approaching, and it is not sustainable for me to respond to weekly calls from motels that you are kicked out of or to save you from risky and unsafe positions you are in due to being kicked out.

Kaylen, I love you, and will support your sobriety and other healthy goals. Please call me from your room phone to let me know best time to connect with you tomorrow (this Saturday) and to confirm your recovery and treatment plan for continued housing subsidy support by the family.

Love, Your sister—

October 2018

My dear sister Kaylen:

This is a gentle reminder that you must be in treatment to receive financial assistance, including dad's housing subsidy. All requests for money are to come through me. Treatment includes UAs. Weekly UAs were discussed and at one point you stated you would go twice a week to prevent relapse; however, the pattern as of late has been every three to four weeks which is not conducive to recovery or preventing relapse. Other conduct that is not conducive to addiction recovery that requires amends include:

> Missed, rescheduling and late appointments: Your attendance at addiction treatment appointments on time is essential for your recovery. Sure, "shit happens" (as you put it), however missed, rescheduled and unpunctual appointments is the standard for you, and it has affected your relationship with your treating physician to the point that he called me last Friday to advise he is on verge of firing you as a patient due to several tardies and missed appointments. You may recall that absenteeism and unpunctual behavior was the same basis for which the intensive outpatient facility placed you on a behavior contract. The enclosed battery-operated clock and calendar are gifts from me so you can enter your appointments and set an alarm to keep your addiction treatment appointments.

> Lost/stolen phone: It is unwise (and arguably unsafe) to maintain company with people that steal your stuff. It is unlikely that mom and dad will pay to replace stuff that keeps getting stolen from you because you are with people who do not respect you or your stuff.

> Lack of communication, unkind/offensive or misleading communication: The last couple of occasions we have communicated or connected you have either not showed, not answered texts (or

calls), yelled at me, accused me of things that are not true (disloy-alty, snooping) or emotional extortion (to support others that I am unable to—for whatever reason that may be). It is unfair and difficult for me to have a relationship with someone who engages in that behavior. Let's develop a kind way of communicating.

I know this month must have been hard with all the turmoil surrounding your spouse. Please know there is understandable res-ervation about your health, wellness and recovery including missed appointments, infections and unsuccessfully meeting minimum treatment expectations. Perhaps setting goals to participate in a more stable treatment and recovery program and kind communication with your family is all that is doable right now. In closing, you are my only biological sister, I care about you, I love you, want to have a healthy relationship with you and pray for successful recovery every day.

Love—Sissy

November 2018

Dear Kaylen,

It is with a heavy heart that I write this letter of apology to you. I'm afraid my involvement in your recovery has not been helpful and rather has enabled you and overstepped what is your responsibility. It was wrong of me to participate (directly or through managing the process) *your* recovery because it is your story of recovery to write, not mine, and your journey, not mine. You have declined and closed the door and second story window on my offers to take you to the hospital and doctor for your obvious need of medical attention for the addictions that grip you, and so I will now step away.

Although my offers to assist and support you in the form of moving you from the streets to varying locations every two to three weeks and weathering unsafe parts of town and snowstorms to drive you to appointments. Invitations for meals, weekends and holidays together and gifts were extended with love and in an effort to healthfully assist you on your journey to overcome addiction and re-write your story and the next chapters of your thirty-something life. I feel, however, that my efforts have served to extend the suffering and harm that stem from the severe substance use disorders for the past several months.

Please know that I am no longer available to you unless and until you are committed to what every addiction and medical professional has recommended for "severe opioid and amphetamine use disorder" and that is an out of state inpatient treatment facility to treat the strong addictions that control and possess you.

Please know that because treatment for severe opioid and amphetamine use disorder has not been maintained, nor has a UA been supplied in nearly a month, I am not authorized to provide housing subsidy.

Kaylen, I will always love you. I wish to help in a non-enabling way. Until the time you commit to out of state inpatient treatment, I pray for your wellness and recovery every day and wish you peace.

December 2018

My dear sister Kaylen,

For the past several months I chose to be in your life to support your decision to treat your severe dependence on drugs and get your life together and on track. Sadly, the last several months have confirmed that your ability to commit to treatment and recovery from drug dependence is in vain, and my endeavors to support you have been unhelpful. It is with a heavy heart that I write to clarify the boundaries of our relationship. The only reason I am in your life right now is to confirm you are in treatment and to supply rent funds.

The last couple of months have been dismal, causing me to step away from you. Indeed, participation in two forms of treatment was insufficient support for you on the road to recovery. Additionally, your addictions and continuous unstable and unsafe housing conditions, coupled with inappropriate and hurtful behavior, is exhausting. The positions you place yourself in are not conducive to recovery, and things you say and do have damaged our relationship. I was sad when you stood me up (again) for a weekend getaway trip. I was physically pained when you closed the window on me as I stood outside in the snow observing needles and foils at the place you are now staying, waiting to drive you to a doctor appointment so that you would not be fired as a patient, and I was emotionally dejected when you raged at me over the phone calling me a bitch and distrustfully accusing me of controlling you and your treatment.

You are distracted from caring for yourself by other crises which include your husband's criminal antics, his consequential jail sentence and your landlord's problems (stolen tools, needs money and apparently verbally abuses you and refuses to meet his end of the rental agreement). It is a statutory breach of the rental agreement for heat not to be supplied in a rental unit. You won't even medically address obvious injury to your leg that has festered for over a month and is bound to get infected in the cold, dank place where you currently live. It is apparent you are still using, and I will not expose myself or immediate family to that injuriousness.

I was hopeful that you would be well into recovery by now, in time for the holidays and your 36th birthday, so that our sister relationship and your relationships with our parents, your brother-in-law, niece and nephew could be restored, and you would have greater support in your recovery and goals in the new year and the second half of your thirties.

Kaylen, it is your job to take care of yourself. It is your job to treat your addictions and recover. You complain that you have zero dollars, and your unemployment and food stamps expired. Perhaps get a job. If you can't get a job, evaluate why that is and how to address the barrier(s). I will not respond to your claimed needs beyond the quid pro already established of housing subsidy/rent for treatment unless and until there are solid signs of recovery, including consistent plan for treatment, clean UAs and a blueprint for recovery and independence from the addictions that grip you. Dad wants to a see a clean UA before another housing subsidy is provided, so that means a clean UA on or before January 3, 2019, for January housing subsidy to be authorized.

I hope and continue to pray that your commitment and focus to treatment of your drug addiction and recovery takes a turn for the better. I love you very much.

~ Sissy

December 17, 2018

My dear sister Kaylen,

This letter follows the recent housing crisis and series of relapses over the past several months and to convey feelings of being misled and deceived into paying thousands of dollars in housing subsidy. First, I am not authorized to subsidize housing any further this month and we are reluctant to provide continued housing subsidy as those funds have repeatedly been squandered into your use of drugs. This recent crisis overset the subsidy by several hundreds of dollars. The agreement requires modification, as this is not the first time our housing subsidy has supported a drug flop house where essential services are not supplied, you are beaten, abused and your property (most of what was again supplied to you by your family, including medication, clothes, blankets and food) is stolen.

Additionally, a clean UA has not been supplied for several months, which indicates lack of participation in treatment and repeated relapses. We understand relapse is part of recovery, however, it appears that your commitment to treatment has been abortive and noncompliant with the housing subsidy agreement. Our parents will not subsidize your addiction nor pay for unsafe housing that fuels your addiction. I am unable to support you emotionally or otherwise unless and until a sustained commitment to treatment by you occurs, evidenced by clean UAs.

It is encouraging that you got yourself into a medication management provider to administer Suboxone. Your attendance at NA meetings are steps in the right direction. Hopefully, your regular attendance and participation in NA meetings will supply a healthier community to support you during the difficult times that addiction entails. It is heartening that you coordinated therapy. Dad and mom support your desire for individual counseling and are willing to pay for the therapeutic services she provides you on a direct billing basis. So, you may move forward to set up an appointment with her and advise how to coordinate direct billing of her services to our parents in care of the office.

Please know funds will no longer be supplied for Suboxone outside of what is prescribed. If the Suboxone that is prescribed to you is lost, stolen or someone else picks up your prescription, that is your problem to solve. Additionally, neither mom, dad nor I will pay your co-pays; those are your responsibility. Perhaps secure part time employment to meet your co-pay and other personal expenses. It is a reasonable goal to have some form of employment.

Starting this January, and until March, dad will agree to subsidize your housing at a set rate *provided* clean UAs are supplied. It is your responsibility to supply clean UAs to me in order to receive the housing subsidy. If you choose to cohabitate and otherwise continue a relationship/association with Kyle when he is released from jail, housing subsidy will cease unless Kyle has a job and pays half of the rent; then dad will subsidize housing at an adjusted rate. You are encouraged to apply for financial support/housing subsidies from community programs for safe, stable and affordable housing. If you have a job and sustained negative UAs with continued treatment, dad will pay half your room rent.

Kaylen, I love you and honor your strength to get back on the horse to take steps toward sobriety. I continue to pray for you and your wellness and look forward to receiving a clean UA in the New Year if not sooner.

Love, Sissy

May 2019

My dear sister Kaylen,

It's been nearly five months to the date of my last letter to you. It's nice to write you under your improved health, housing and anticipated employment circumstances. I have also enjoyed our sister-connection times that have allowed for emotional support and for our relationship to grow closer.

In these past five months you have achieved so much! As an initial matter, congratulations on "coining out" of the intensive outpatient program. The family is pleased with your independent effort at addressing your addiction, including coordination of your latest participation in rehab, containing housing and transportation expenses, getting yourself to and from treatment, NA meetings, job interviews and employment.

I write to get on same page about further financial subsidy by the family. As has consistently been the rule, sustained sobriety (supported by clean UAs) and employment is necessary for continued subsidy, and contribution to your living expenses is needed with establishment that you can afford to care for self and your dog.

We are all so very proud of you. You are on your way.

Much love, Sissy.

Glossary

Active Addiction: When a person is currently using drugs or alcohol.

Addict: A person who is addicted to a particular substance, typically an illegal drug.

Addiction: The fact or condition of being addicted to a particular substance, thing, or activity. Chronic releasing disordered characterized by compulsive seeking of continued use behavior despite harmful consequences and long-lasting changes. It is considered a complex brain disorder and mental illness.

ADHD: Attention Deficit Hyperactivity Disorder is a mental health brain disorder that affects behavior and how a person pays attention. Symptoms may include inattentiveness (easily distracted, not finishing tasks or following instructions, forgetfulness, inability to organize, loses things, daydream) and hyperactivity (excessive talking, squirms or fidgets, always moving) and can include mood swings, impulsivity and evolve into anxiety and depression.

Al-Anon Family Groups: Mutual support program for people whose lives have been affected by someone's drinking.

Bargain: An extension of denial that includes making promises or compromises that allow continued abuse of substance of choice in exchange for token changes of behavior.

Boundaries: Defined rules or limits established to protect security and well-being with and around others that are identified and expressed how other people behave to feel healthy and safe.

Chugiak: An unincorporated community within that Municipality of Anchorage, Alaska. This Alaskan community settled in the 1950s primarily by homesteading by military personnel that served in World War II. The term is said to have come from a Dena'ina Athabascan word that means "place of many places."

Co-Dependent: Excessive emotional or psychological reliance on a partner, typically one who requires support on account of an illness or addiction.

Crack House (also called crack den): A place where cocaine in the form of cracks is bought, sold and smoked. Usually blacked out windows and unclean with overflowing toilets, spoiled food, stained walls, peeling wall paper, dirty and damaged floors scattered with trash, glass pipes, tin foil.

Denial: Also known as the **denying phase**. A coping strategy referenced in Kubler-Ross Five Stages of Grief. Denying helps the aggrieved survive by not living in actual reality and living in a preferred reality.

Detachment a.k.a Detach with Love: Step back, away from and separate from the loved one's addiction. It is a letting go of someone's addiction for them to experience the consequences of addiction and allows you to focus on your own well-being. As they say, "It's simple but it ain't easy."

Detox: Short for detoxification. A process or period of time in which one abstains from or rids the body of toxic or unhealthy substances.

DOC: Short for Drug of Choice, see below.

Dope Sick: Slang for opiate withdrawal symptoms typically experienced when detoxing from pain killers. Symptoms vary depending on DOC and can include nausea, headache, achy body.

Drug of Choice: substance abusers preferred drug, informs clinical picture for diagnostic purposes.

Eighty-Sixed (86d): A term establishments use to cut off service, asked to leave or remove self from the premises immediately.

Enable: To give someone the authority or means to do something. In the recovery circles can include providing the addict money and means to support their habit, including shelter, paying bills for them, downplaying the severity of the problem, lying on their behalf to shield consequences, rationalizing behavior or making excuses for them and behavior that delays the moment the addict is forced to confront the full gravity of the situation.

Fix (also called hit, rush): Dose of a narcotic drug.

Flophouse: Place that offers low cost lodging, space to sleep and minimal amenities.

Framily: Friends that are family. Online urban dictionaries define it as a blend of friends and family that are close and choose to be related because the relationship is mutually respectful, close, and supporting. We include the favorite people in our lives in our family, whether they are blood related or not, because we love them.

Heroin: Highly addictive drug derived from morphine, often used illegally to produce euphoria.

Intervention: The action or process of intervening, interference in another's affairs, action taken to improve a situation, especially a medical disorder. A carefully planned process that may be done by family and friends in consultation with a professional to have an effect on the outcome.

Interventionist: An individual who helps identify the appropriate people in the life of a person who is experiencing substance use, mental, or behavioral health problems that is part of the recovery team.

IV: Acronym for intravenous. Administration of fluids or medication directly into a person's vein.

Junkie: Slang for a person addicted to narcotics, and especially heroin. A person with a compulsion habit or obsessive tendency.

King Pin: Leader of a crime syndicate who rules. A main or central person essential to the success of an organization or operation.

Lawyers Assistance Committee: A group of lawyers that promotes the well-being of the legal profession and protects the public by providing education, respectful confidential assistance and referrals for lawyers that are members of the Bar, their families, colleagues, and clients affected by a member's mental health and substance abuse issues.

Loving from Afar: Loving someone you cannot be with either because they are toxic, unhealthy, or there is a negative energy. Freeing yourself so that this love will materialize into something more. For me it was caring for someone without feeling obligated to take care of them.

Methadone: Used to treat opioid use disorder, pain, narcotic drug addiction, and commonly to treat heroin addiction to reduce overdose from street drugs. Can be used short- or long-term to reduce cravings and withdrawal symptoms. Can be used over several days for detoxification or extended use for maintenance therapy. Usually taken by mouth, rarely by injection. There can be side effects and risks with taking this medication.

Morning Wellbeing Time (MWBT): Acronym for Morning Well Being Time.

NA: Narcotics Anonymous, a support group for those attempting to recover from drugs in recovery, a group where people recovering from drug addiction can help each other pursue healthy choices.

Nar-Anon Family Groups: An anonymous spiritual program based on the Twelve Steps of Nar-Anon for those who are affected by someone else's addiction that know or have known a feeling a desperation concerning addiction of someone close.

NARCAN: a medicine that reverses opioid overdose. Used nasally in overdose emergency. Real name is Naloxone. Every state has different laws, but generally available for purchase at over the counter drug stores. Narcan can be free from community health services or visit the National Institute on Drug Abuse.

Narcotic: A substance used to treat moderate to severe pain, not made from opium, that acts like opiates and called opioids.

Overdose (OD): Ingestion or application of a drug or substance in quantities much greater than recommended. An overdose may result in a toxic state or death.

Recovery: Abstinence from drugs or alcohol.

Red Flag Feelings (RFF): Toxic and hard mindsets, moods, feelings, or emotions that destroy or don't serve well. Fear, Guilt, Anger, Resentment.

Rehab: Slang, short for rehabilitation. A course of treatment for drug or alcohol dependence can be an inpatient facility or outpatient.

Relapse: Recurrence of a past condition, deterioration after a period of improvement. When a person stops maintaining a goal of reducing or avoiding alcohol or drugs.

Rock Bottom: The lowest possible level. A point where things cannot get worse.

Safe Crack House: Although illegal in most areas, some cites maintain a house run by non-profit organizations that maintain safe injection sites for heroin, opioids, or other drugs

Score: Purchase drugs.

Strung Out: Physically debilitated, stupefied, intoxicated by a drug. Addicted to a drug

Suboxone: Narcotic opioid medication that treats narcotic dependence. Prescription needed.

Substance Use Disorder (SUD): A mental disorder that affects a person's brain and behavior, leading to an inability to control their use of substance such as legal or illegal drugs, alcohol or medications. Symptoms can range from moderate to severe, with addiction being the most severe.

TAYL: Acronym for The Addict You Love.

Trafficker: A person who deals or trades in something illegal.

Trap House: Originally used to describe a crack house, a drug house, shelter for drug users, and place for dealers to supply. People who lack stable housing may call a trap house home as it's a place for them to find shelter. Trap houses are a drug dealer's base of operations and shelter with constant supply of drugs for users. Users are trapped in the house. Trap houses can be abandoned places, beautiful homes, basements of decent family homes, rooms in hotels or motels, or AirBnBs.

Trapped Out: Being associated with a trap house or residential environment dedicated to the distribution to the sale or distribution of narcotics.

Treatment: Intended to help addicted individuals stop compulsive drug seeking and use. Can occur in various settings and take various forms and lasts different lengths of time due to relapses from the chronicity of the disorder. Drug treatment can include medications, behavioral therapies, or a combination.

Trichotillomania: Drug use can increase hair pulling compulsion as a coping strategy for stress, anxiety, and obsessive related psychological conditions.

Trigger: Something that affects your emotional state causing overwhelm or distress, may present as crying, unexplained anger, increased anxiety, or panic.

Tweeker: Slang for a person who illicitly uses methamphetamine. The term was coined due to sleep deprivation addicts usually undergo.

UA: Acronym for Urine Analysis or Urinalysis. A test of urine to determine the presence of illegal and prescription medications.

Withdrawals: Physical and mental symptoms that occur after stopping or reducing intake of a drug the characteristics of which depend on the drug that is being discontinued. Symptoms can include anxiety, fatigue, sweating, vomiting, depression, seizures, and hallucinations.

Acknowledgements

My anchor and caring husband Christopher, our fierce, understanding and patient daughter Grace and solidly sweet son Connor for the support each of you so uniquely and individually provided.

To Auntie Mamie for being awesome. Cousins Kell and Isaac for staying up late and holding me through the phone line through some of the battles. Auntie Shee-bee for reminding what a champion is and that I am never alone.

Julee for everything, including adopting Gus. Leia for your courage. Marie and Hayley for your professionalism and support at the office.

To my girlfriend posse in effect, each of you brought your own dance moves to this life party and have made it worth living. My first friend and reader, Sharon who stands with me at church, holds me when I cry, and sang with me and listened to my vent sessions. Life-long friend Kyra who loves me from afar in a different way and confirmed to me in person there is no shame in attending support group meetings. Stephanie for holding space, for being a first reader, and being there at the right time and place. Kathy for being a first reader and present in the scary world of detox and withdrawals, and for taking me to my first meeting. Natalie for being a first reader and sharing stories; your edits to my letters and the gifts of hand-made cards used with love. Tammy for walks and talks to process and sort whether I am in the real world. Lesley for reminding me that crying is courageous. Rennya for standing strong with my over-giving, tender heart tendencies. Shelly Belly for being a first reader. Shanda for lunches, dinners, and meet ups with our sons to confirm that we are not alone in our crazy and it is okay to leave it untucked sometimes. Mary for being a first reader, supportive and understanding in so many ways. Marlo for introducing me to anger, conjuring the ability to sit and be with her.

John Hanrath for working deeply with my family, especially my parents. You made an impression. I still have your card. Julia and Jon Marc for being legal angels, kindly receiving my calls, gently holding space for me and being a navigation system through "criminal land." Peter who validated that it is okay to pray for divorce. John, Doug, and Jim for being there at the right time. David for taking my call, listening, sharing your experience, providing help line information, and John's contact number.

Managers at the motels and treatment centers for being real and honest. *Sister Siren* team of writing coaches including Valerie Costa copy editor, Christy Day book designer, and Annie for her designs, I appreciate your patience.

About the Author

MICHAELA KELLEY CANTERBURY is a lawyer and writer. Michaela obtained her J.D. at Gonzaga University School of Law in Spokane, Washington, and graduated from Duquesne University in Pittsburgh, Pennsylvania, with a BA in political science and a minor in philosophy. Michaela is licensed to practice law in Alaska and is owner, operator and lead trial lawyer at Kelley & Canterbury LLC, where she works with her husband, Christopher; partner in all things. Michaela resides in Eagle River, Alaska with Christopher, where they raised their son, daughter, and dogs in the same valley and woods where she was raised.

Made in United States
Troutdale, OR
11/15/2023